How To Get
*What You Want When You Want It
Where You Want It in the
Way You Want It
Through Numerology*

WESTERN SYMBOLOGY

By

JULIA SETON, M.D.

"THE RALLY,"
9, PERCY STREET,
LONDON, W.1,
ENGLAND.

COPYRIGHT 1933.
By "THE RALLY."
(All Rights Reserved).

PRINTED IN ENGLAND.
BY BIRCH AND WHITTINGTON, EPSOM.

Kessinger Publishing's Rare Reprints
Thousands of Scarce and Hard-to-Find Books!

We kindly invite you to view our extensive catalog list at:
http://www.kessinger.net

WESTERN SYMBOLOGY

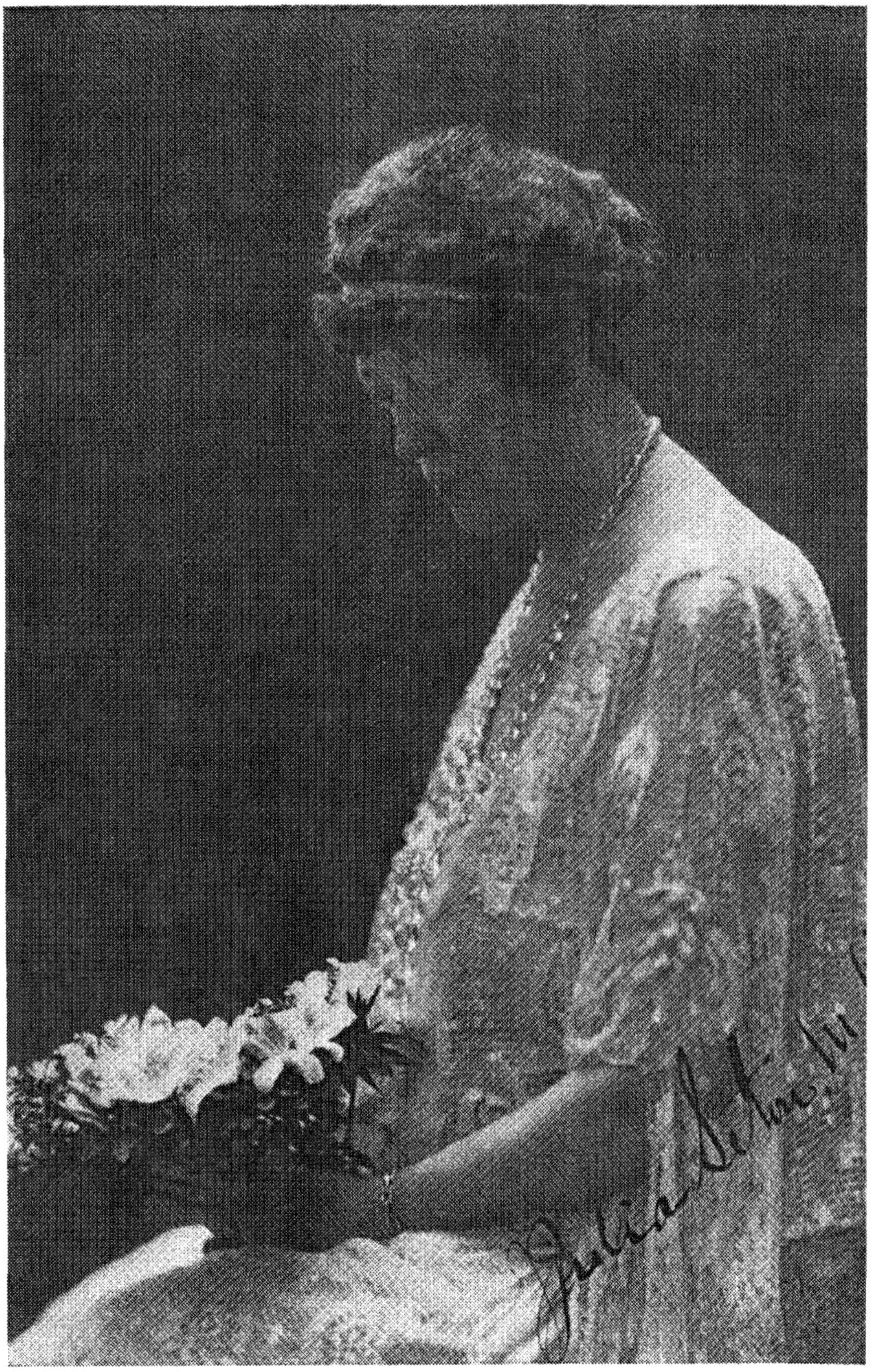
Julia Seton

DEDICATED TO HER WHOSE LOVE MY LIFE HAS BLEST—MY DAUGHTER, DR. JUNO BELLE WALTON

CONTENTS

PROLOGUE .... PAGE 13

BOOK ONE

THE EYES OF TRUTH

CHAPTER
- I. WHAT IS NUMEROLOGY? 21
- II. WHAT ARE NUMBERS? 23
- III. MYSTICAL INTERPRETATIONS 25
- IV. HOW NUMBERS AND LETTERS CAME 27
- V. WHERE OUR NAMES CAME FROM 31
- VI. COSMIC VIBRATIONS 37
- VII. THE ONE, THE MANY, THE ALL — THE MOTLEY THRONG 43
- VIII. THE GREAT PARADE, OUR PLACE IN THE THRONG 44
- IX. THE NOVITIATE (THE ONE) CONSCIOUSNESS, THE FIRST DEGREE: THE 1-2-3 45
- X. THE INITIATE (THE MANY) CONSCIOUSNESS 47
- XI. THE ILLUMINATI (THE ALL) CONSCIOUSNESS, THE THIRD DEGREE: THE 8-9-11-22-33-44-55-66-77-88-99 49
- XII. THE FOUR LIFE VIBRATIONS OF OUR TRUE SELF—PERSONALITY, SOUL, DESTINY, INITIATION 52
- XIII. THE TRUE SELF: OUR PERSONALITY 52
- XIV. THE TRUE SELF: OUR SOUL 55
- XV. THE TRUE SELF: OUR DESTINY, THE COMPOSITE SELF AND THE VOCATION SYMBOL 59

7

CONTENTS

CHAPTER	PAGE
XVI. THE TRUE SELF: OUR INITIATION, REBIRTH AND OUR NINE INITIATIONS	62
XVII. THE GREAT WITHIN AND THE GREAT WITHOUT—THE INTROVERT, THE EXTROVERT, THE SUPRAVERT	70
XVIII. THE GREAT WITHIN, THE INTROVERT	71
XIX. THE GREAT WITHOUT, THE EXTROVERT, AND THE SUPRAVERT	72
XX. THE GREAT LAW OF PERIODICITY, CYCLES	79

BOOK TWO

THE LOVE STORY OF THE WORLD

XXI. LOVE, MARRIAGE, DIVORCE	91
XXII. COMBINATIONS FOR TRUE LOVE AND HAPPY MARRIAGE	93
XXIII. MARRIAGE FAILURES	97
XXIV. CAUSES OF UNHAPPY MARRIAGES, THE LAW OF OPPOSITES	98
XXV. TYPES OF INHARMONY	100
XXVI. COMPLEMENTARY MARRIAGES	105
XXVII. THE SECRET IN MARRIAGE NAMES	108
XXVIII. WEDDING DAYS, HOW TO START TOWARD THE THINGS DESIRED	111
XXIX. WEDDING HOURS	116
XXX. MATCHING SYMBOLSCOPES FOR MARRIAGE	118
XXXI. HOW TO NAME CHILDREN	120
XXXII. THE FIRST AND LAST LETTERS OF NAMES	124
XXXIII. THE CIPHER VIBRATIONS	126
XXXIV. INTENSIFIED NUMBERS	128
XXXV. PLANETS AND NUMBERS	130

CONTENTS

CHAPTER		PAGE
XXXVI.	PET NAMES AND THEIR MEANINGS	130
XXXVII.	THE RULING PASSIONS OF HUMANITY	132
XXXVIII.	THE RULING PASSIONS OF MEN — BODY, MIND, SOUL, AND SPIRIT	135
XXXIX.	THE RULING PASSIONS OF WOMEN—BODY, MIND, SOUL, AND SPIRIT	150
XL.	PERSONALITY, OR WHAT WE LOOK LIKE	168
XLI.	SPECIAL NUMBERS	180

BOOK THREE

THE PSYCHOLOGY OF SUCCESS

XLII.	THE PLANES OF EXPRESSION	189
XLIII.	POSITIONS FOR VOCATIONS	191
XLIV.	NUMBER COMBINATIONS IN BUSINESS	198
XLV.	YOUR NUMBERS AND YOUR VOCATIONS	204
XLVI.	"LUCKY," OR CONSTRUCTIVE NUMBERS	209
XLVII.	"UNLUCKY," OR RECONSTRUCTIVE NUMBERS	215
XLVIII.	ELEMENTAL FORCES	216
XLIX.	THE MALEFIC SYMBOLS	218
L.	HOW AND WHEN TO CHANGE A NAME	225
LI.	SITUATIONS, PLACES AND THINGS	233
LII.	THE MYSTIC POWER OF GEMS, COLOURS, AND FLOWERS	236
LIII.	HOW YOUR YEARS ARE NUMBERED — THE CYCLES OF THE BIRTHDAYS	237
LIV.	HOW TO ADJUST YOURSELF TO ANY YEAR IN HEALTH, HOME, AND BUSINESS	240
LV.	YEAR BY YEAR	243
LVI.	THE MONTHS	252
LVII.	SUMMARY OF MONTHS AND YEARS	253

CONTENTS

LVIII.	PERSONAL ACTION IN THE YEAR	255
LIX.	HOW TO SET ANY COMING EVENT	258
LX.	HOW TO ATTRACT MONEY	262
LXI.	BUSINESS SIGNATURES	264
LXII.	POSITIVE AND NEGATIVE NUMBERS	265
LXIII.	HOW TO WRITE A SYMBOLOSCOPE	270
LXIV.	HOW TO INTERPRET A SYMBOLOSCOPE	274
LXV.	YOUR KEYNOTES, HUMAN CHORD, AND LIFE SONG	281

BOOK FOUR

A SOUL'S REFRAIN

LXVI.	THE LAST WORD	284

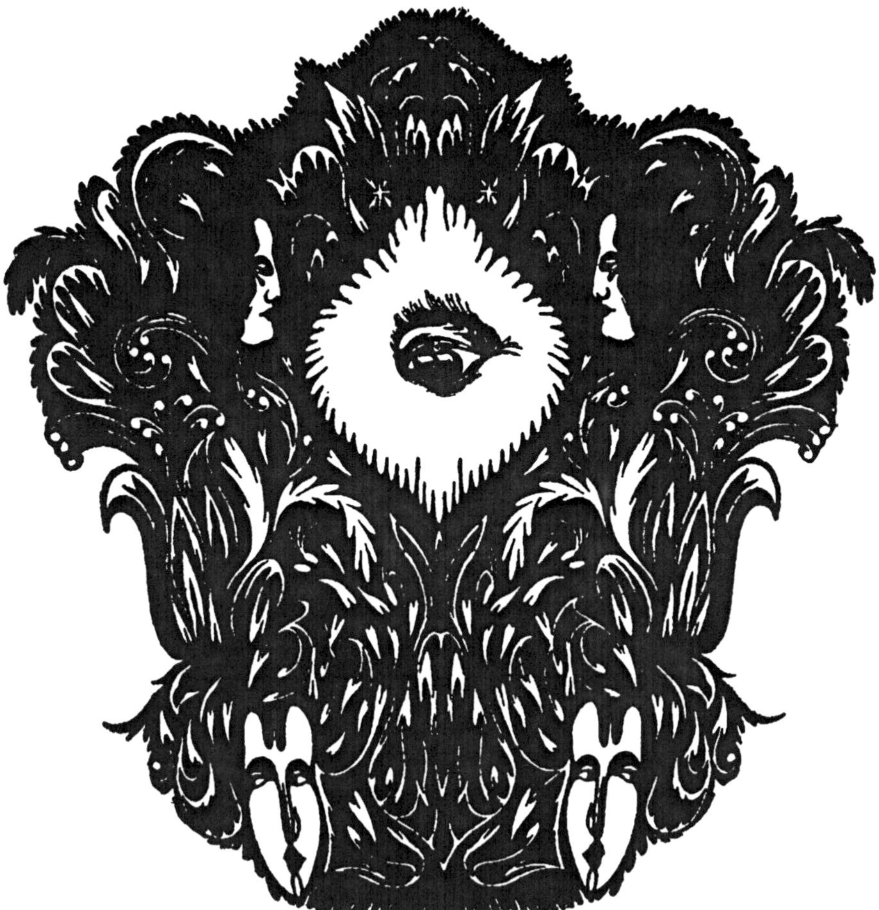

PROLOGUE

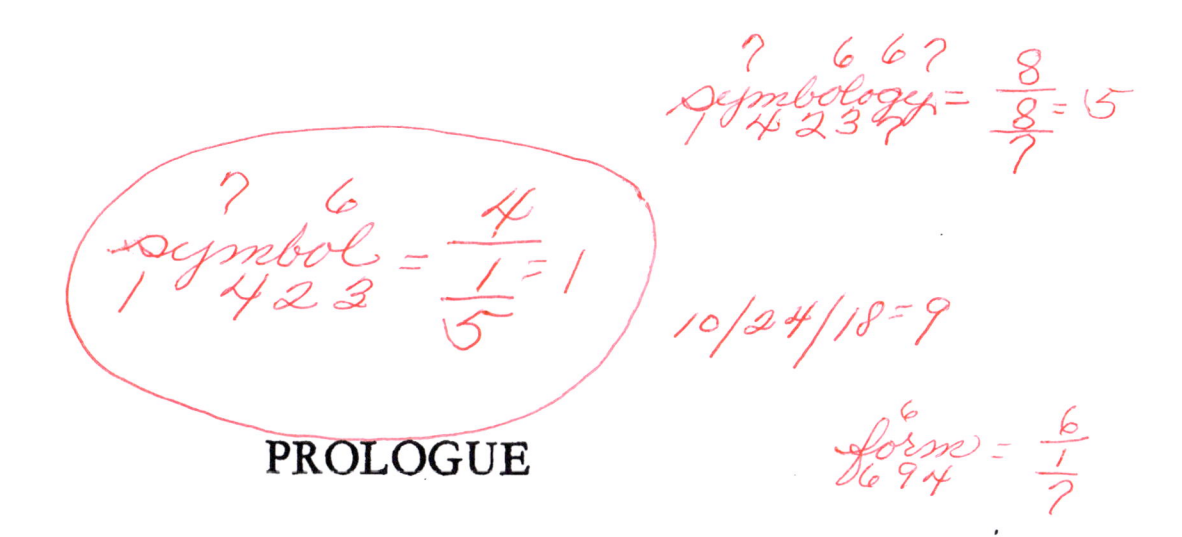

LIFE is revealed to us through symbols—there is not life outside of form. If we can correctly read the symbology of the things we see, we are seers; and, through this, conquerors.

This book is written for those who are eager to read and to understand their *own* symbology, and the symbology of people, of situations, and of things.

There are many who will not pause to read symbology. It has no language they can understand—they are content to take life as they find it, uninterpreted and just a confused bundle of states.

These can wait until their own experiences send them on into a deeper questioning. But to the tireless toiler up the hills of life, symbology becomes the rod and staff which comforts and leads to the truth that reveals and the mysticism that explains.

We cannot always resist the inner urge to know ourselves. Eventually we must ask why, where, when, and how subtly to follow that which is seen, back to the invisible Source from whence it came.

How do we know that the things we say in this book are true? We know because we have four kinds of evidence:

First. We have the authority of those gone before us, who have weighed, balanced, and explained the forces of life in action. They have left the result of their researches an open book for the enlightenment of those who might come after them and seek to find, as they had sought.

Second. We know through our own personal experiences in life. We have found these things true for us. We did not make them; we found them demonstrated every day, and in every way. They confronted us, and we had nothing to do but to apply them to our own situations. Experience is a dear teacher.

Third. We know by the experiences of others. Although we pity and strive to help, we know that not one jot or title of their own law will pass away if they go on in a vibration which can bring only its own things; if they do not change they are hopeless. Too often we have seen that which does not permit us to doubt that as soon as they change their methods and vibrations, everything changes. By establishing our ignorant vibrating contacts, sickness, poverty and misery came into the world. By our very own consciousness must come resurrection. Knowledge is power.

Fourth. We know, because life itself has been our teacher. Life itself has written an answer to every human questioning; and he who runs may read when he has developed the vision that does not deceive him.

We live in a world of unquestionable law and order, in which everything has a meaning; and this meaning must be made plain at some time. When it is understood it brings to us a divine content.

The burdens of ignorance whip us all into wider reaches of our consciousness—we cannot choose but go on, once the pain of stupidity and the urge of escape have infected our minds.

To help to find the true self, to help to find the true way to live, to help to find love, and, through all these, to find God, is the purpose of the symbology of this book. There is herein a well-wrought way of thought, word and action, which, if not actually final, at least offers a trustworthy guide to our origin, privileges and destiny. Thus, we can find the truths of life itself that will bring us into tranquility, non-resistance, self-realization, and infinite union.

The truths in this book are not obscured or hidden; they are not entangled in a maze of words and impossible calculations. But, a simple story of all human relationships is told, showing how these relationships may be used in sane, sensible, spiritual living.

J.S.

I have Books to fight against the "pain of stupidity & ignorance" "Knowledge is power"

There is no Golden Rule of all ages
But some blindfolded fools have called it brass.
There's no beatitude of Wisdom's pages
But some have sworn its jewels were but glass.
Stand forth, O Truth! Strike hands with those
Who face with faith the new, all dawned and
    pearled!
When men shall hail All Truth as neighbours—
    not
As foes—under the Great Charter of the World

—Anonymous.

BOOK ONE

The Eyes of the World

BOOK ONE

THE EYES OF TRUTH

I. WHAT IS NUMEROLOGY?

NUMEROLOGY is the science, philosophy, psychology and religion of life interpreted from the symbols of names, dates and numbers. It is modern alchemy with the power to bring forth from two well-known substances another almost unknown compound which is easily interpreted and registered because of the perfect reliability of the original compounds.

Pythagoras said, " God geometrizes." We are all named, chorded, numbered and placed in the great eternal plan of things. Numerology is the primary explanation of the symbol of this placing. It is primary from the fact that it deals with gigantic cosmic principles in so simple a way that even the simplest mind can understand and apply them.

Numerology is cosmic science reduced to human facts and explained in human words. It has an unmistakable relation to human thought, deeds, words and experiences. It interprets man to himself. It shows him the why and how, the when and where of his environment and his situations in this environment. Man finds that he is a great universal equation, and numerology shows the part, the place and the time.

With this we answer the question of where, why, whence and whither, because we find where we belong in the cosmic whole. We find our origin, our privileges, our destiny. We find what we have at the back of us, within us, and ahead of us,—the secret of our present condition, and it may be explained sensibly.

Numerology points to the book of the past, present and future through the history written in our symbols. We find that we are not in time alone, but in eternity. What we build today we take with us into the future. Our yesterday, today and tomorrow are one.

Numerology, with its symbol-lessons, scientifically reveals in what grades we stand as human beings, and opens a door through which we can escape from good to better and on to best. It helps us to live our everyday lives as masters and not as slaves. We find the lines of least resistance for success (material power), name, place and freedom; we find also the subtle cues that give us peace, wisdom, worship and service. We find the answer to our happy and unhappy marriages; the answer to holy and unholy living. Its wisdom comforts us in our errors, and helps us in our aspirations.

Numerology began when life began, because in the beginning there was the ONE. It will last while life shall last because the ONE was made FORM and became the MANY which, in each part, has the **essence** of the ONE.

Alchemy, geometry, symbology, numerology—these make the square of all truth that has been or ever will be. Translated into simple language for the understanding of the human mind, they constitute one of the great revelations of this century.

Races will come and go, but truth translates itself again and again. " It answers not, it does not take offence, but with a mighty silence bides its time till men shall turn to it with glad surprise."

II. WHAT ARE NUMBERS?

NUMBERS are the symbols of the place and arrangement of the planes of intelligence in the universe—the index cards of Divine Intelligence.

The planes of intelligence are LIGHT, AIR, FIRE, WATER, and EARTH, which give us the sky, air, fire, water, and earth realms.

The ebbing and flowing of the tide of life between these realms gives us what we know as universal intelligence, in form and action. The flow is with men (the personal); the ebb with the GODS (the universal).

This circle of the Infinite is a clear pool in which the sky and earth, or the upper and lower things, are reflected and registered. The whole upper expanse the Ancients called heaven; the lower expanse they called earth.

The registrations or reflections of substance are named, numbered, colored, and chorded in this planet we call the *world*. Humanity was forced into numbers because in the beginning was the One, then the registrations began and the Two appeared—the first pair,—which was the duality of Oneness and the commencement of universal geometry.

This duality is always pressing in upon humanity and demanding explanation. It forces the earth vibrations and elements to recognize the upper realms, and, at the same time, it compels the upper side of life to make itself felt in the lower or earthly side.

As we become more and more aware of the Two-in-One and of all that we might attain through understanding the laws of unity, we are compelled to compare the many angles of life. It is then that the table of registrations begins.

It is a part of the universal plan that all vibrations must work together for the final perfection of *all*. The lower must include the *higher* and the higher must be found active in the *lower*. Thus humanity eventually finds that heaven and earth are one.

Every vibration (or registration of intelligence) in the universe is part and parcel of the same substance, only moving at different rates of activity. Humanity bears the image of the earthly and the image of the heavenly. When it awakens to this understanding of itself, and can translate all life into numbers, it can then read the riddle of the Sphinx and is " twice-born."

III. MYSTICAL INTERPRETATIONS

ALL the elements of intelligence in the universe combine in registrations of 1, 2, 3, 4, 5, 6, 7, 8, 9, 11, 22, 33, 44, 55, 66, 77, 88, and 99.

1

ONE is the center of union of all these vibrations. ONE is the real I AM of all humanity, the centre through which all illusion and matter are linked with the rays of all other realms.

10

TEN is the registration of the evolving grade—the last bridge between lower and higher intelligence or the bridge between earth and heaven.

2

Two comprises some of both. It is the double standard—a man standing with one foot on earth and one on the borderland of heaven. He may easily lose one or both.

3

THREE is the combination of both and the next step upward, possessing the characters of both and can easily be either angel or devil.

4

FOUR is the square of heaven and earth—the complete Adamic man. From here he starts into the next vibration, carrying the whole world on his shoulders. If he falls, his own world fails utterly.

5

Five is the conscious extension of the earth ray into the upper realms of spirit. The Adamic man's earth mind is completed in 4 and in 5 the holy link is consummated.

6

Six is the balancing number vibration of light. *Six* must color all matter with light. It is that light which shines in the darkness and lights every man that comes into the world.

7

Seven is the withdrawal from the Adamic man into the heavenly One, the beginning of complete realization of the upper vibrations. It is the " dweller on the threshold " of heaven, fearing to look back.

8

Eight is the balancing point with matter, and is the first true form in the world of light.

9

Nine is the final crossing of light with matter, or the last union of mortality and immortality. From 9 we reach the bridge of

10

Ten between heaven and earth, over which we pass to 11, the complete dual ONE, and are ready for the new birth or to become " twice-born."

It will be interesting to remember all of these mystical interpretations when we come to consider the meanings of numbers and vocations. No matter how much the outer situations, people and things refract these vibrations, the subtle power of the mystical and occult carries right on with them, working their way into the objective just as the force behind a rose pushes it into bloom.

IV. HOW NUMBERS AND LETTERS CAME

NUMBERS are always symbols of the definite co-ordination of the elemental vibration in the universe. They are simply the registrations of the *cosmic vibrations;* they tell the pulse beat of all life. The great cosmic currents beat *in* at the vibrations of 1, 2, 3, 4, 5, 6, 7, 8, and 9, and they complete each vibration in 11, 22, 33, 44, 55, 66, 77, 88, and 99 throughout all space.

These vibration currents must have form, and *letters* are the bodies of vibrations with which we can register and interpret the vibrations of *our* being and of the universe.

Combined together, certain vibrations give most distinctive expressions. Others are less important, but every vibration in form means something and gives its own quality of power.

The biggest life is that which includes and concentrates the most vibrations; and the perfect life is that which expresses constructively for itself and for others the things it includes.

There are *twenty-six* letters in our alphabet, and they are combined in many different ways in the names of people to express their qualities of consciousness; but, in whatever way they are arranged, they are the true symbols of the individual's self-hood.

Naturally there must be duplicate numbers or there could not be 26 letters. The ancient interpreters gave us a table of nine vibrations through which these twenty-six vibrations move and around which we arrange the alphabet according to each individual.

WESTERN SYMBOLOGY

1	2	3	4	5	6	7	8	9
A	B	C	D	E	F	G	H	I
J	K	L	M	N	O	P	Q	R
S	T	U	V	W	X	Y	Z	

Anyone including and expressing the constructive vibrations of any number becomes the finished product of that number; and the letters of our names tell us plainly where we stand in power or weakness.

There are dramatic, artistic, religious, executive, constructive, political, philosophical, scientific, physical, mental, emotional, psychic, and spiritual numbers. As individuals we can judge the true qualities of ourselves and others by the preponderance of any of these numbers. A name made up of a great number of the weaker numbers would be noted for its weaknesses, surely not for strength; the body of its vibrations would limit the owner in the direction of greatness. A name made up of power numbers would displace weakness and give boundless opportunity for perfected self-expression. A name formed of letters of an artistic nature would not lend power to practicality, and a name formed of the symbols of practicality would not tend to give artistic or dramatic art.

The greater the number of letters in a name, the more complex are the vibrations of consciousness, and the more difficult it will be for those having many letters in their names to live poised, calm lives and keep harmonized along definite lines of action. Unless they understand their ruling passions they can easily become the discordant playthings of their mixed vibrations. The life of Joe Hann is not as complex as the life of Sylvester Augustus Epsworth. The problems of life and action do not disturb Joe as greatly as they do Sylvester. There are very few things that Joe will have to do in life; but Sylvester, with all his vibrations, has a big contract to work through.

In the final expressions of consciousness, and in the highly developed, the number symbols become more and more reduced; only a few symbols are needed, and these express the full self. It is often noticed that men in their early lives use all their names to show their place and position, but when they become established in some one thing they use only one name, and this name includes the full and complete expression of their consciousness and character. When they become established they can express all of themselves to the world through one name, as Edison, Marconi, Selfridge, Lincoln, Ford, Washington. When they become a well-known fixture, they can be easily reached by simply addressing them by one name to their particular city, as Fields, Chicago; Childs, New York; or Lyons, London. It is not necessary to include the street and number or other information.

All consciousness, when concentrated and expurged, becomes simple, and not many numbers are then needed to tell the tale of the self. The complex is always in a state of unfoldment, and many names and long names mean a long list of unfinished experiences. "Wisdom walks with us in crooked ways and tries us until she can trust our souls." When our souls can be trusted, all these many experiences are not necessary, and our desires are too concentrated to bring us so many symbols.

We are really only seeking happiness. As we get older in growth and experience, we find that only a few things are needed for our happiness, and that we can choose the methods of thinking, acting and speaking that will bring us these things we desire. Thus, we

WESTERN SYMBOLOGY

narrow down to the few number symbols that contain all we require. The path of life is from simplicity to simplicity, and our names and numbers keep pace with this law.

Our names with their numbers tell us what states of consciousness we have brought with us. We can work out each one laboriously or we can put them all in one big sweep of consciousness and take all our experiences through the few.

No matter how long our names may be, we always find that our intimate friends shorten them. Thus they require us to put forth only a few vibrations to please them. *James* often becomes *Jim* and this lets Jim live three vibrations instead of the five in James. *Robert* becomes *Bob*, and only three vibrations are used instead of the six in Robert. No matter how far we may go in our personal experiences, the law of life is to drag us back to the REAL, and in the REAL we need emphasize only a few important symbols. We can escape many of the lesser things in this way—just as the full swing of the stream rushes all the débris along with it.

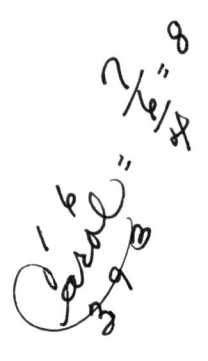

V. WHERE OUR NAMES COME FROM

In the beginning, before human consciousness was specialized, men knew each other only by the qualities of character they expressed. Names first originated from what was seen and heard and felt. Names came in the past, just as they often do now, from the qualities in the person or thing itself and the effect which is made on others.

Because men could find no beginning and no end to universal life, they made a circle to symbolize its continuity. When they could find no end to distance, they made a straight line. They found distance crossing in space and time, and from this crossing they found centralization and direction and called it east, west, north and south, contained in one.

When men fished all day they were named fishermen. When they hunted all day they were called hunters or huntsmen. When men would not fish, hunt, nor work, but loafed around all day, they were called setters. When they gathered faggots or wood they were called woodsmen. When they were surly and mean they were called bears or bearmen. When they carried great loads on their backs they were called camels or camelmen.

No matter how far away names may be from their original roots, they always carry with them some trace of what they were in the beginning. All names and their numbers are simply symbols of consciousness in the individual. A name is our shield and buckler; by it we rise or fall; in it are all our guideboards to show us the way to our ultimate destination. Every name, and every letter of the name, is a signboard along the highway of our journey which says, " Turn to the right."

It has often been found that if a child is allowed to go without a name over a certain length of time it will name itself. Quite young children have been known to give themselves very wonderful names. Often, when a child has grown into adult life, it will change its name of its own volition, letting go of one or more of its general names, or selecting the one which is the most popular with its friends or parents. Pet names often come in this way.

Many things have been named and afterwards the use of the thing itself causes the public to rechristen it.

Here is a little item from a daily paper, which shows that even the most uninitiated have stumbled onto some part of the truth:

" They say a rose by any other name would smell as sweet, but, like so many other trite sayings, is it really true?

" There is often inspiration in a name. The best names do not come from taking thought. They flash out from inspiration. A new and nameless article or commodity needs a name. There are two ways of naming it. One way is to sit down and coldly invent a name, solving the problem as one would a cross-word puzzle or an acrostic. Such a name will lack inspiration and poignant descriptive quality; race horses and Pullman cars are named that way.

" The better way—and speech itself has evolved from this way—is to let the new thing suggest its own name. It will have a dozen impalpable qualities mutely yearning for verbal expression. Give the novelty its own way and likely as not its name will come from some entirely unexpected quarter, from some humble employee, or from a friend of somebody within the establishment. But that name will fit—it will more completely bear witness to the quality of the commodity itself than any later combination of descriptive words that can be invented. The rose had to be called a rose because it smelled so sweet."

There are many people who find that they have lived up all the experiences their name indicates; they then naturally change their name. Sometimes this is done by rearranging the letters of their own name; sometimes an entirely new name is selected.

Every change and rearrangement of our name means a different period of unfoldment. The nature of the new unfoldment is indicated by the vibration in the numbers of the new name, or by the cessation of the old vibrations we have discarded. When we have enough of anything, we can quit; and the determined and conscious selection of a new name indicates that we have finished some old grade and are ready for new experiences.

What's in a name? Just the whole story of the self from the beginning to the present, with the potentialities of the future. Names can be made the trade-mark of fame, opportunity, privilege and honor, or they can stand for all that is infamous in human character. Jesse James is as notorious for crime as Johnnie Walker is for whiskey. Napoleon is the symbol of power; Joan d'Arc was the symbol of the light and courage of inspiration; while Francis of Assisi was the most Christian of Christians.

No one is ever really alone in life, for our own name symbolizes our higher consciousness; when we understand it we use it as a lamp to our feet. And, in the long, long way that we must walk through the experiences which our life brings us, we can trust it to guide our steps aright.

Here is another clipping taken from a daily paper that gives interesting and amusing information concerning names. It is worth perpetuating for all numerologists. The author is unknown.

" With respect to the English-speaking world it may be pointed out that not until a period between the years 1050 and 1250 were people called anything more than plain John, William, James or Richard. There was nothing in the world by which to indicate who the kin were or to what family they belonged. Surnames had not yet come into vogue.

" A man was in those days in constant danger, so far as his life went, of getting lost in the shuffle and about the only way for a family to keep together was to go through life holding hands. It was this condition that gave rise to the surname, a sort of family trademark, that linked one to his own immediate folks. Surname, derived from the French surnom, or over-name, was written over the given name. Some authorities, however, contend that the word was originally ' sire name ' or ' father's name.'

" Before that time, unless one had some personal peculiarity, or had accomplished something to distinguish him from his fellows, he was just one pea among a lot of peas. If he chanced to be noticeably brave, he might happen to be known as Richard the Lion-Hearted. If he was tall, as well as bowlegged, he would probably be dubbed either Edward Cruickshanks or Dick Longfellow.

" But this crude scheme was unsatisfactory to the plain nobody, who was just like everyone else, so the surname solved the problem of locating the Johns, the Williams, the Richards and the Henrys. Instead of saying such a one was the son of William, that everybody knew, he was referred to as William's son, and all of William's children, no matter whether they were sons or daughters, were known as Williamsons. And so it was that the names of Dickson, Peterson, Thomson, Stephenson and a host of others, came into existence. The Scotch and Irish followed the same plan, the word ' Mac ' meaning son, being affixed to the father's name. Hence we get the MacDonalds, the MacHenrys, the MacDavids and the like.

" For a long time the Welsh stuck to the old custom of distinguishing a man as the son of his father by the use of ' ap,' as Alexander ap Howell, but this proved a cumbersome method, as it did not always indicate clearly just who a man was. Some other Howell might have a son named Alexander, and so there would be two Alexander ap Howells. So sometimes it was necessary for one to sign the name of his grandfather and even of his great-grandfather before he could get himself properly placed. For instance, Alexander ap Smith ap Jones, ap somebody else, clear back to the seventh or eighth generation. By the simple expedient of dropping the ' a ' in ' ap,' we have Powell, Pridmore, Potter and Price, mere modifications of ap Howell, ap Ridmore, ap Otter and ap Rice.

" Many of the Christian names of that time were retained as the family name, or surname, and we at once think of the numerous Henrys, the Lewises, the Charleses, the Franks and the Andrews. Our ancestors did not seem to be at all averse to advertising their callings by adopting them as surnames, hence the existence of Messrs. Shoemaker, Sadler, Skinner, Tanner, Cook, Weaver, Spinner and scores of others.

" Many of our forebears were employed in the homes of the nobility, and the surnames of some of them to-day tell us exactly what their duties in the household were; there can be no doubt in the world where Mr. Kitchen, Mr. Hall, Mr. Butler, Mr. Stairs or Mr. Garrett laboured. Many surnames are but the telling in one short word where the first of the family lived, as is instanced in such names as Woods, Fields, Brooks, Hill, Marsh and many others that one can readily recall.

" In other times shopkeepers did not put their names over the doors, but hung a sign that bore some strange device. This might be a bird, a beast, an insect, a fish, a flower, or something else in the realm of nature. So it was easy to adopt the object on the sign as a family name; as a consequence we have the host of Birds, Harts, Lyons, Drakes and Cranes.

" Then, too, one's personal appearance, his gait, his peculiar disposition, the colour of his hair, or a hundred other characteristics, might have had much to do with the naming of a man. It may have been in admiration, or it may have been in derision, that a particular name happened to be tacked on a particular individual, but they have remained with the family all the same, through thick and thin.

WESTERN SYMBOLOGY

And so we have the great company of Longs, Walkers, Singers, Whistlers, Doolittles, Whiteheads, Lightfoots, Armstrongs, Blacks, Whites and Browns. Just because a man's name happens to be Lord, Duke, Earl, King, Bishop, Abbot or Knight it does not necessarily follow that his ancestors were any of these, as it was a custom, in many instances, for one employed by a member of the nobility to adopt the title of his master as a family name. If one's vocation called for the striking of blows on metal, he was a smith; and as there were blacksmiths, goldsmiths, silversmiths, locksmiths, coppersmiths, it is no wonder that to-day the world is running over with Smiths."

THE EYES OF TRUTH

VI. COSMIC VIBRATIONS

THERE are just three things in the world, and these are intelligence, action, and form. Action is vibration or cosmic movement, atomic, molecular, mass. The study and control of intelligence in action and form is *Alchemy*. This, divided into its cosmic parts and consciously arranged and rearranged, is *Geometry*. These parts, known and classified, constitute *Symbology;* and the symbols named, numbered, coloured and placed, constitute NUMEROLOGY.

There are just five cosmic forms in which intelligence acts. They are the root-forms of all subsequent division. All vibrations originate in these five forms, and there is nothing in all the world, seen or unseen, that is not in these elements.

The five cosmic forms are light, air, fire, water, and earth. Light is the first form of intelligence in action and earth is the last. Between these pass all the other elements. Stepped down to its ultimate, light becomes earth, and earth stepped up becomes light. " All things come newborn from light; all things return reborn to it. In light all existence is."

These five vibrations blended, become cosmic substance. And, moving at different rates of motion, they are that of which all worlds and the things in them are made. There is no substance outside of these elemental intelligences of *light, air, fire, water,* and *earth*. Their endless combinations go on working their way into the lily, the dynamo, the coal and the diamond, the desert, the forest, the reptile, the horse, the dog, and the man, " each form bringing forth of its own kind whose seed is in itself upon the earth."

The first amalgamation of all this intelligence produces the mineral kingdom; the second, the vegetable kingdom; the third, the animal kingdom; the fourth, the kingdom of man; the fifth, the angelic kingdom; the sixth, the atmospheric kingdom; the seventh, the kingdom of Etheria; the eighth, the Manasic kingdom; the ninth, the Nirvanic kingdom, or the kingdom of perfect self-realization.

Streaming from east to west, and west to east, north to south, and south to north, these vibrations of light, vibrating high and low, and slow and fast, form every mineral in the mineral kingdom and every differentiation of form in the vegetable, animal and human kingdoms.

A man is man, and not a mineral, vegetable or animal, simply because through countless ages, cosmic substance has flung itself on from atom to mass until it has power to manifest itself in the form called *human*.

" Dust of the earth, shot through with mystic gleams,
　Brief whiles of glow, with inklings of the God,
Mind and soul, alight with star-fed dreams,
　Thy hope fulfilled—Man sprang from out the sod."

There is one universal intelligence in all and through everything seen or unseen. We call this intelligence Spirit or Mind or God, because it is the animating principle of all life. The ancients taught that this intelligence formed all things, was in all things, but that in itself it was more than the things it formed. This intelligence, even while it produced the universe, remained more than the universe because it was not only the created things but the thing creating—and the creation.

THE EYES OF TRUTH

This Spirit is the center of everything, and the form emanating by its force and from its substance is the Spirit of Life, always bringing forth of its own kind. This Cosmic Spirit is the heart of the flower, and the life of everything on earth. Those who found this said:

" I am not lonesome nor apart
  That men should say, ' Lo, there:'
I am the all—immersed in all,
  Behold me everywhere!"

" There is a Spirit in man and the inspiration of the Almighty giveth it understanding." This Spirit in us we contact familiarly as our mind, and through this we are related to the Universal Mind, or Spirit. Every vibration of Cosmic Spirit or Mind embodied in our human form shows forth some refraction of the Universal, but the way with which we manifest it is known as the Self, and by this Self we are identified.

In this sea of moving intelligence called Life, the atomic mind is always vibrating into the currents of 1, 2, 3, 4, 5, 6, 7, 8, 9, and 11, 22, 33, 44, 55, 66, 77, 88, 99—never changing, never slowing, never speeding, but repeating again and again in duality double 1 or 11, double 2 or 22, double 3 or 33, and so forth. " As it was in the beginning, it is now and ever shall be, world without end." This is the Pool of Siloam in which we all wash and " come out seeing."

If this pool were water and we stood on its edge and dropped a pebble into its depths, we can easily imagine how the ripples of the water would run out and toward its circumference. Then let us suppose we drop another pebble at an increased rate of force, and still another and another until we had plunged nine pebbles into the pool, each increased in force until the ninth had included the force of all those that had gone before plus its own momentum.

In this pool, the ripples would seem to our eyes to move in an incalculable tangle; we could not see where one began and another ended. Yet, in the very plan of cosmic geometry, each ripple and the symbol and the number of itself would be intact. If we knew how, we could trace each motion to its original source.

This is the symbol of the sea of life in which we live and move and have our being. " Life has many tangled pathways, joy has many shades of woe; lights and shadows, softly blended, hide deep things we do not know." Just so, we, in our own living, mingle, tangle, untangle, amalgamate, and seem to lose much that is our own; yet, like the true passage of the wavelets, we never lose our own identity but somehow remain eternally one with the Source of our original selfhood.

The mineral kingdom with its many ripples of substance forever remains mineral, the kingdom of man, remains mankind. The intelligence inhabiting it passes on and upward into finer form. There is always this permanent intelligence, inhabiting millions of forms, impermanent to it. It outgrows them and builds more stately mansions, but remains ever itself in the great scheme of cosmic form.

The mineral, vegetable, animal and human are always permanent stations in the eternal life. But the ego man, or the spirit man, is always a passenger, taking his own time en route, always on a personally conducted tour, breaking his journey, passing on again at will. The ego man changes through experience, expression and inclusion, which brings a larger intelligence, and this larger mind seeks new form for its finer manifestations.

The ego man must go on, but he leaves unharmed the things through which he has come and in which he has played his part. A higher degree of intelligence will naturally arrange a higher environment for itself as it passes through substance.

We find, then, that the highest kingdom of vibrating intelligence in form is man; at this point creation on earth stops. Man stands, in his kingdom, the apex of the creation; and, standing here in supreme vibration, he becomes master of all the vibrations in the kingdoms beneath him and of the kingdoms themselves.

Man is the distributing center, and he cannot choose but to broadcast himself into the pool of intelligence in which he is. He drops the pebbles of thought out into the seething mindless mind and his world begins to form around him. He is the central point of his own pool, and the fountain of his thinking cannot rise higher than its source.

He soon finds himself encircled with his own thought vibrations; his thinking space becomes filled with ripples which mix with the ripples of the thought spaces of his kind. And here he begins to seek to read the riddle of himself, his mind, and his world.

His thinking spaces become filled with the substance in form of his own consciousness. His vibrations sent out link him with the vibrations of the universe, and he makes contact consciously with the One, the Many or the All, and in these he finds the relationships of 1, 2, 3, 4, 5, 6, 7, 8, or 9.

We must forever take our place in this great " Pool of Life." We must forever *make* our place the measure of ourselves. We make our places through our own thinking and acting; with what measure we mete it is meted to us. The universe does not care whether we are

2, 4, 7, or 9, but we will soon find that *we* care, and that there are vibrations which it is well never to set in motion, and with which we may well refuse to contact.

In this pool there are positive and negative vibrations that build up and send on, and also vibrations that tear down and reconstruct. We can turn this waiting substance into the ripples of hate or love, joy or sorrow, health or disease, wealth or poverty. No ripple comes back to us but the one we send out.

When we truly find ourselves, we can read the story of the vibrations we have set in operation for ourselves; we read them through the symbols we find in our names and birth dates. Not one jot or tittle of the law will pass away, and what a man sows he must reap. Life hangs our story in the skies, the stars, our features, our hands, our colours, our *symbols* and our *numbers*—and he who runs may read.

VII. THE ONE, THE MANY, THE ALL— THE MOTLEY THRONG

In the beginning was the ONE, and, dividing, this ONE, became the first pair. The first pair produced the third, and thus the first trinity came. The trinity produced another ONE, which was the quaternary. Out of this quaternary came the whole human race. Humanity stood foursquare.

Humanity is just one great throng of moving, human beings, black, red, brown, yellow, white. While they are mixed together in the throng, like threads in the woof of some old loom, there run the mixed strands of the half-caste world.

Humanity began when life began. It is not a part of universal life, or a creation in it, or a projection from it, —it is the unversal life itself, embodied and expressed as human beings. We are deathless souls on an endless journey. Life is from beginning *to* beginning again.

In this great motley throng there are three divisions into which all black, red, brown, yellow and white people enter somewhere, play their parts, and take to themselves the fruits of their own actions and reactions. These divisions are the ONE, the MANY and the ALL. This is the great human trinity, the eternal procession —never ending—going on and on,—symbols of the paths of life. Each one is in his allotted place. No one sends him onward, but himself. No one holds him back, but himself. All power lies in the crypt of his own consciousness, and is legible to himself when he can read the handwriting on his own walls.

Somewhere all people enter in and take their places, play their parts, and claim all that belongs to them through consciousness, efficiency and colour. Within every human being of any mixture of colour are the impulses of his own desires. This constitutes the God-push within driving him on to all final attainments.

If we can look with the larger vision, we see that all these races and half-castes are separate and distinct, even while they seem to be hopelessly involved in the tangled skein of life, in kaleidoscopic colours and mixtures.

VIII. THE GREAT PARADE

OUR PLACE IN THE THRONG

WHEN we reduce all the vibrations of the universe to final vibrations, we find that they may all be interpreted by 1, 2, 3, 4, 5, 6, 7, 8, 9, and their doubles 11, 22, 33, and so forth. Therefore we say there are *nine* great cosmic virbations in which we live, move, and have being. Each one of these vibrations has its own individual meaning. When we come to consider the meanings of numbers it will be well to memorize them very thoroughly, for upon their meanings depend the ultimate qualities of the self.

IX. THE NOVITIATE (THE ONE) CONSCIOUSNESS

THE FIRST DEGREE: THE 1-2-3

IN every race, or mixture of blood streams, the 1-2-3 are wholly concerned with self. They are not definitely interested in anything which does not concern some line of their own affairs. Individualization is their keynote, and individualization is a hard lesson to learn. It is hard to become so magnetized that we can attract to ourselves the things we want, and conquer and control, and, at the same time, keep so close to the universal law of justice that we do not destroy others in our progress.

The *first* lesson the ego man has to learn is to own his own soul, and to make it consciously an integral part of the whole world of people, situations and things. With self-ignorance all human life begins; and with self-realization all human life must finish.

Those who are individualizing in Grade One never worry about anyone but themselves. This is one of the reasons they are called selfish. It is not really possible for anyone outside of the One vibrations to accurately measure the impulses of those in the One because they are moved by impulses of self-preservation which are totally unfamiliar to minds in the other vibrations.

While we are vibrating to the impulses of One, we are concerned solely with our individual wants. What do we want? How do we want it? Where do we want it? And what do we not want, and how, and where, and why? There are just two things to a One consciousness, and these are the things that make *for* them and the things that make *against* them. There is no middle path for 1-2-3.

Self-preservation is the first law of nature, and this is the ruling passion of those who move in the consciousness of the One. We are, then, in an exclusive state of mind,—never knowing that if we lose our life in one thing we must find it again in another; that life never takes one thing away but something else is given.

When we are in the department of the One, we spend our money for our own pleasures. We have little interest in things in which we have no part; all roads run back to us. Everything in life increases or decreases in value according to the degree of pleasure, comfort, freedom, or success which it affords us.

One is the first great grade in the school of life, for in it we learn the I Am. Go into any race and watch and listen and you will find these dwellers of the first grade. Many live and die in it, never realizing that it was only one of the grades in the big school. Those in the other grades often cover it with censure, forgetting that it is themselves as they were yesterday, and that it is only a small part of life—only a place where we stop until we can stand up and say: " I am the divine thinker of my own thoughts."

The One is the degree called the Novitiate. A Novitiate is one who does not know, does not know that he does not know, often thinks that he knows, and almost stops his own progress by his ignorance.

Sometimes he seems like an Ishmaelite with his hand against every man and every man's hand against him. But life sends him on through experiences which his own dominant thoughts and actions bring upon him; and love and duty influence him until he grows out of the natural states of mind of the One and knows that if he is really true to himself he cannot be false to any man. Then he goes on to the next grade to sink himself into the Many.

X. THE INITIATE (THE MANY) CONSCIOUSNESS

THE SECOND DEGREE: THE 4-5-6-7

THIS is the grade in which we lose our personal self-consciousness to find it again in the lives of others,—their interests are our interests, and we can only reach our own ultimates through helping others to reach theirs.

In this grade we are apt to take a great deal of pride in what we call our unselfishness, but which is not really unselfishness at all but just the method which our fuller inclusion has adopted. It is still self-realization, but a realization mingled with others.

Working for others is to the 4-5-6-7 just another way of self-satisfaction. It gives us more happiness to find ourselves in others, and their happiness is our greatest happiness. It is only a higher delight and one of life's finer forces.

In the division of the Many we sink self more and more into race consciousness, the home, the state, the country, national affairs, internationalism, society, organizations, clubs, lodges, universities, colleges, hospitals, and all that tangles us up in endless skeins of human interests.

The Many are at that stage of unfoldment where they cannot accept anything for themselves that is not for the good of the whole human race. Pride in self-abasement is as great as the pride we felt in our own individualization. As we did not recognize our selfishness in the stage of One because it is a part of the great plan that we shall be self-contained, just so we do not realize that we are lost in the Many because it is a normal point in true self-development. There are many who live and die in this stage of unfoldment and never know that it is only a grade in the ascent of consciousness. They do not know that when we have concluded the lessons we go on, not because we will, but because we must; for when resistless change is powerless to aid, it must mar. We are on our journey Godward, and it is not a part of the Divine Plan that we should stay too long in any grade.

Life is a means to an end,—God-consciousness or consciousness of All. *Almost unconsciously we grow into a wider vision through the pressure of the experiences which our submerging brings to us. We include in our being all the wisdom of the One and the Many,* and are ready to go on into that class of Illuminati where we work through great finals.

The *Many* are called *Initiates*. An Initiate is one who knows that he knows something, but he knows there are many things which he does not know, and he is eager to learn more and more of the mystery of being.

XI. THE ILLUMINATI (THE ALL) CONSCIOUSNESS

THE THIRD DEGREE: THE 8-9-11-22-33-44-55-66-77-88-99

THE third grade is the one of *universality*—the All in All. Here we have privileges unknown to us in the other grades. Wisdom has walked with us in crooked ways and tried us until she can trust our soul; and we are out into the understanding and power we have won through experience and observation.

It is written, " There is no ' Thou shalt not ' to the Illuminati." Here we find ourselves free to do what we ought to do without being told; and we are judged by life according to deeds done. We are fully individualized; we are a conscious entity in the heart of the Infinite. We have been submerged and lost in the race-consciousness and have emerged—plus. While still dwelling in the mass world, we know that we are more in it than of it. We feel that we are like visitors in a world in which we have very little part; and yet, in it we have all—everything we do, think, or say reacts with fourfold energy.

We have been redeemed out of the *part* into the *whole* without losing anything but our sense of belonging. Working always in the part with perfect self-realization, we learn that he who finds himself loses his misery, and that from the alone to the alone is the real path of the human soul.

In 8-9-11-22 we find that we are individualized gods

on our own self-created pathway, that we cannot lose our own, and our own is just what we create for ourselves through thinking, speaking and acting. In 8-9-11-22 we know that all loss is gain, that nothing can be taken away but something else is given, and we can say truthfully, " Not mine but thine."

The Illuminati knows, and knows that he knows; he knows what he knows and how he knows, and works from a certainty. He is all things to all men, and his higher efficiency puts him beyond the plane of competition. He knows his work and can do it. He does not battle with any weaknesses; he only strengthens his strength.

The Novitiate does not yet know—he *thinks* he knows. The Initiate *knows that he does not know* and seeks to know. The Illuminati *knows that he knows*. This is raceology, and, when interpreted, number-symbology reveals the place and power of our very being.

When we study our names and numbers, it is a revelation to us to find in which grade we belong. If we have many numbers of the One we know the basic thing in our character; and if there are many of the impersonal or universal numbers, we can, with all these symbols, translate ourself to ourself.

It makes a great deal of difference in our daily contact with life and its changes where our weight of consciousness falls. If it is in the One we will act like One and colour all life with the view of the One. If it is in the Many, we can be sure we will act like the rest of our crowd. If it is in the *All*, we will be in the world, but not of it. We will know each type by the things of their division. The watchword of the One is " I—I—I," of the Many it is " Ours—We—Us," and of the All it is " Thine not mine."

There are no comparisons possible between these great divisions of place and consciousness. They are simply different—neither good nor bad, but each is perfect for its type. A perfect One is as good as a perfect All or a perfect Many. The only difference between any of these divisions is the different way in which they respond to the influence of life. Their conduct will bear the prints of their development. " By their fruits ye shall know them," and they all bring forth of their own kind.

AN EXAMPLE OF NOVITIATE-INITIATE-ILLUMINATI

H a r r y   R i c h a r d   B l a k e
8 1 9 9 7   9 9 3 8 1 9 4   2 3 1 2 5

NOVITIATE	INITIATE	ILLUMINATI
1,3,1,2,3,1,2	7,4,5	8,9,9,9,9,8,9

This registration shows that Harry is fairly well balanced between the Novitiate and Illuminati qualities of consciousness, with the weight on the side of the Illuminati. We can read by the small number of Initiate symbols that he is not much of a questioner. His problems are solved for himself. He does not argue or explain—he is sure that he knows.

The Novitiate numbers give us the clue to the way he would express his Illuminati conclusions. He would be very positive, sane, creative, and not likely to be turned aside from his own opinion or his own method, after he had once arrived at his own conclusion. He would be right, and those around him would soon find that his practical methods were best because he had illumination at the back of them. He could afford to be laughed at for his ideas because he would know in his heart that " Those who laugh last laugh the loudest," and he would be sure to have the last laugh.

XII. THE FOUR LIFE VIBRATIONS OF OUR TRUE SELF

PERSONALITY, SOUL, DESTINY, INITIATION

IN order to study ourselves individually, we must divide ourselves into four separate parts, and then determine from the vibrations of each just where we are in the universal plan and just what vibrations we are intensifying. These four divisions of ourselves are:

1. Personality *(The sum of the consonants)*
2. Soul   *(The sum of the vowels)*
3. Destiny   *(The sum of the vowels and consonants)*
4. Initiation   *(The sum of the day, month and year)*

XIII. THE TRUE SELF: OUR PERSONALITY

PERSONALITY gives us the clue to what is back of us—our past experience—and this is found by the *sum of the consonants* in our names.

Everyone has latent possibilities which can be awakened under provocation and when we are born we bring with us some of the positive vibrations of our past life. We all have lived in qualities of consciousness so long that we have built them into form. We can say, "He looks like a farmer," "She looks like an actress," or "He looks like a business man." All of which shows that we have emphasized these things in our lives until we have set them into our personalities.

THE EYES OF TRUTH

Our personalities, when inharmonious, are proof positive that our past lives have been unhappy and not lived in peace or harmony.

The secret of beauty of face and form is found right here; and if we come into the world with everything in our favour and good looks, it is because we have given these things to ourselves in the past by thinking, speaking, and acting along the lines of higher harmony and rightness.

It is said, " Beauty is only skin deep," and there is something true in this, for the qualities of consciousness which built our personality may not be the active ones in this life. We have finished these and must take on other initiations. So, while we may look like a saint in face and form, we may have a very negative expression of the other part of the self—the inner man.

It is very important to know what is back of us, for then we know we have powers which can be called upon in an important moment. It is really the wisdom of our past lying dormant, and it often stands us in good stead when a crisis confronts us.

The vibrations of the personality can become a great stepping stone to success, for when we learn our best power vibrations, we can tune the personality up to its very best expression, and win by its attraction. Some people neglect the personality, and then wonder why they never make good contact with people and situations. The truth is, that personality is a great asset, and everyone anywhere, including all business concerns, woud rather look at pleasing than unpleasing people.

Even if our past has been such as to cause us to bring over an ugly personality, we can make it charming and step it up to its very best by knowing what we have at the back of us to depend upon.

A PERSONALITY EXAMPLE

Harry Grovenor

It can be seen that this name contains nine consonants. Taking the numbers of these consonants:

```
H r r y        G r v n r
8 9 9 7 = 33   7 9 4 5 9 = 34
```

the sum of the numbers in each name, and reducing 33 and 34, to their final digits,

$$33 = 6 \qquad 34 = 7$$

We add these digits together (6 + 7) = 13, which, reduced to a single digit, equals 4. So we find that Harry Grovenor has at the back of him the essence of 4, and when we remember that 4 means strength of character, power of organization, and mental leadership, with controlling and directing power and the ability to remain steadfast to responsibilities, we know just what Harry would do under pressure.

The qualities of the vibrations we have at the back of us are our reserve stock which we can call upon in emergencies. So Harry will never fail anyone, but can do a great deal more than many might think he can, for they have no way of reckoning the latent forces of his character unless they are numerologists or occultists. We need not add the 33, but we find that the character is the same. Read carefully " What 4 Looks Like."

XIV. THE TRUE SELF: OUR SOUL

THE vowels of the name reveal the *soul*-power. They are the symbols of our *real self*, and the heart of the ego called man. Adding the number of the vowels in the name and reducing the result to a single digit reveals the character and quality of our true self. " As a man thinketh in his heart, so is he; " and " Where his heart is, there his treasure will be found."

Glowing like coals upon some sacred altar fire—never darkening but flaming out again and again through eternities—this great Cosmic Flame localizes and expresses, and is, within man, the Spark Divine.

This Spark Divine is the ego, or the true self. When we consciously reach this Spark Divine within us, we are out to the land of the naked vision and the single eye, and we stand face to face with the Infinite in the Finite. Arriving here, no man returns; it is the Tableland of the Soul; " and he who finds himself, loses his misery.

Where our hearts are, our treasures are, or, in other words, our desires are. These desires in us constitute the law which brings us out into the vibrations that satisfy us. If our soul is 9, we may be sure that our love and desires are in the things and situations of the 9, and just the same with other numbers. We cannot be a 4 at soul without loving the things of 4. A 5 in soul is forever seeking the things of his own desires; where they are, he is, and where he is, they must be, if he is ever to be happy.

The vowels of any name,
A—E—I—O—U
1   5   9   6   3

WESTERN SYMBOLOGY

carry with them the substance of reality. They tell just the sort of persons we are, and just what may be expected of us under any given circumstances. We will always act according to our soul vibration.

If we have children, we may know by the vibrations of the soul number just what sort of individuals we have to entertain and direct. When we have a large family with different soul vibrations, we will often be at a loss to know what to say and to do for them, unless we know just what they are in the very depths of their beings.

Parents should always know what sort of person they have invited to be their child, and then, as with an honoured guest, give the best to it that they have to give. When they know what their child is, they stand a good chance of satisfying its young desires. (See the chapter on naming children.)

If we take any person in our association at a perverted valuation, it is our fault, not theirs, if they disappoint us. They are just what they are; their vowels have set their stamp, and if we think they are something quite different, they are not to blame. They will act as their numbers indicate, and if we had known them as they really are, we would not have been disappointed.

There are number symbols which tell us of the probability of these qualities of character. If we are too blind to read the handwriting on the wall of every life, we cannot blame others for not revealing it to us.

The vowels of any name, A, E, I, O, U, with their number symbols 1, 5, 9, 6, 3, tell us what is in us, where our treasure is, what we are not, and just how we will colour all our life. This is the eternal Ego, the spark that never dies, but translates itself from century to century. It takes with it into each new birth the essence of its last experience, and this is kept and thrown back into the personality, to be used for sudden emergencies. The best is never dissipated; individuality always has a full storehouse upon which it can call, when at any place on the path, it should face arrears.

The soul of man may meet change—it contacts experience again and again—but in reality it is changeless, even while it is always adding to and casting off. We are, unconsciously, always taking note of this " soul stuff." We often say, " She is a lovely soul," or " He has a kind soul." And many times we say, " The soul of things," or " They have soul-qualities."

Through finer and finer selection we build for ourselves a soul of love, peace, power, worship and freedom.

Taking again:

H a r r y   G r o v e n o r
1   + 6 + 5 + 6 = 18 = 9

The soul number of Harry is 1, which means individuality. As will easily be seen, the sum of the vowels in Harry's full name is 18, which when reduced to a single digit, gives 9. The vowels of Harry Grovenor are, therefore, 9. When we look up the chapter on the meaning of numbers, we find that he is a humanitarian at heart, loving, philanthropic, entertaining, charitable, genial, forgiving, popular, artistic and dramatic.

What, then, is each of us *as an individual?* A friend, a lover, a father, a child, a worker, or a leader—in every line that life touches us? The answer is easy. We are, and always will be, in this life, just what the number-symbols of our soul indicate. These vibrations are steadfast. This is the tiger that does not change his skin and the leopard that does not change his spots.

This is one of the determining factors for happiness or unhappiness in marriage, love and friendship. Where is our soul? There we will find our treasures of love and happiness, and when we find these—the life of our own substance—we find peace.

When we know that anyone has for a soul-number the vibrations of a liar, we can get on with him just as well as if he had an honest number; for when we know that these activities are at work in him we do not expect him to stand for the same amount of soul pressure that another might stand without flinching. We are our brothers' keepers, and it is up to us to know rightly the sort of temperament and character of those in whom we trust.

Our trouble commences when we think a liar is just like an honest man, a libertine like a virtuous one, and a thief like one who, from force of character, could not steal. When we know ourselves and others, we will find an answer to all the problems of the self.

XV. THE TRUE SELF: OUR DESTINY

THE COMPOSITE SELF AND THE VOCATION SYMBOL

THE sum of all our numbers represents our destiny and vocation. It takes all our vibrations to truthfully reveal all our many impulses, and these numbers reveal the plan of the self. We are all pieceworkers and the sum of our vibrations shows the next pattern in our woof.

There is something with which we are busy from the dawn of reason to the grave. Some come to accomplish themselves, some to help others, some just to express themselves, some to learn freedom, and many others come to fulfill the desire for a home. Many are only here to be alone and not lonely. Others come to feel the thrill of power; and still others come filled with divine compassion for the race and busy themselves working for humanity.

If we were to sum up the destiny numbers and the meaning of their piecework, we could say individuality, association, self-expression, service, freedom, home and mother, silence and aloneness, power and position, humanity.

These are the great tapestries of life! These are being worked out in some form as the next step on the path of construction. No matter what our total of composite letters and numbers may be, it is the symbol of our piecework; and, since that is true, it must naturally show our vocation.

The vocation number is the really important number in choosing one's life work. We can earn our living best at the work which is set for us at birth. When we

WESTERN SYMBOLOGY

have come into full relationship with our piecework vibration, our vocation becomes our art, and work is play.

Naturally we all like to do the thing we can do, and it is when we select things that do not belong to our division that we suffer and fail to succeed.

Take three men out of employment who wish to know where they shall go and what they shall do for success. We may find that the soul of all three is 6 and know that where their souls are, their treasure will be, so we could send them fearlessly to any city having the soul of 6. But, when they arrived, they would have to go to work at their own piece of work, if they wanted the highest success. In order to tell them this, we would have to know their vocation numbers, what they were destined to do, and whether their work was of the outer vibrations, or *vice versa*. A person with the inner vibrations of 1-3-5-7-9 will turn naturally to the vocations of these numbers, while one with the outer vibrations of 2-4-6-8 will naturally follow where his interests lead him.

When we know our vocation number and just what we are destined to accomplish in this life, we are free and need not waste any time experimenting with other things. Everybody must work out his own salvation and his piecework must be finished and set in the great spiritual mosaic of industry; this is how we sublimate matter into the form of our own spirit.

A DESTINY EXAMPLE

H-a-r-r-y G-r-o-v-e-n-o-r
8 1 9 9 7   7 9 6 4 5 5 6 9
  34   51
   7 plus   6 = 13 = 4

Thus it is seen that 7, the final digit of the sum of the composite numbers in Harry, when added to 6, the final digit of the sum of the composite numbers in Grovenor, gives 13, which, reduced to a single digit, is 4. Harry Grovenor will, therefore, have a 4 destiny. (See the section on the meaning of 4.)

We find that he can go to any city with the soul of 9 and can engage in any work under the classification of 4. For instance, as an organizer, head or manager of any business, professor in a school or university, musical director, illustrator, bank clerk or manager, salesman, billing clerk, juryman, auditor—all mental positions are open to him.

He has many avenues of endeavour ready for him, and if he fails to live a successful life, there is no one to blame but himself.

All numbers can be classified in this way. The vocation number is the guide to congenial employment; no matter if it is 1, 2, 3, 4, 5, 6, 7, 8 or 9, the vocations of our numbers never fail.

Taking, then, the final digit of the sum of all their letters, we might find that one man is 4, one man 8, and the other 1. We can easily see that any vocation belonging to these vibrations would be the one to seek. When we come to vocational numbers it will be well to study carefully the vibrations of success for the life work. (See section on numbers in relation to vocation.)

The difference in the destiny numbers gives us the secret of the difference in the choice of vocations. One whose vocation vibrations are in the numbers of the inner side, is not in sympathy with the numbers of the outer side or their vocations, but when one's vocation numbers and soul numbers are similar, one's vocation becomes his *art*.

XVI. THE TRUE SELF: OUR INITIATION

REBIRTH AND OUR NINE INITIATIONS

There are only nine cradles for the race and they are occupied by those who come into life fitted to occupy them. It is not possible to get into the wrong cradle—accidents never happen. All life is cosmic law. It must naturally follow that these nine cradles are occupied by the same ego again and again before he learns the initiations of his birth.

We bring our own record and this stamps us forever in our own section. As the sum of all our numbers is called our Destiny, the sum of our Initiation numbers is often called our Fate number, because no matter how we juggle our vibration, we cannot escape the hour, day, month and year of our birth. We must face the people, situations and things that these vibrations bring to us. We cannot escape them, but we can learn to make them minister to our personal success, power, and freedom, or we can let them limit us and delay our life-game. No matter what our fate may be, 1, 2, 3, 4, 5, 6, 7, 8, or 9, we can put our whole weight of consciousness on the positive side, learn our initiation, and come rejoicing.

We choose to be born; we choose the time, the place and the father and mother to whom we are born. All these are symbols of the next experience necessary in our unfoldment. In each new birth we must take on some new initiations even while we repeat some of the old ones at a new level of opportunity.

THE EYES OF TRUTH

The number-symbols of our day, month, and year of birth give us the clue to the initiation through which we must pass, and the people, situations and things we must draw around us in our passing.

We are deathless souls on an endless journey and we must deliver ourselves along the nine pathways of experience, expression and inclusion. The biggest life is the one which includes the most. This is why we find the 9 the most inclusive of the single vibrations.

The vibrations of our birth time set the barriers for this life. We will find that life crowds us right on into the experiences we have come to include. Therefore, we take one initiation after another. *The race is not to the swift nor the strong, but to the spirit of our own application and vibration.*

The initiations of 1, 2, 3, 4, 5, 6, 7, 8 and 9 are all different. They stand alone and will not let the ego pass until he fulfills their demands. These number symbols of our initiation are only the signboards of our path which say, " You must turn here to reach your full development."

Finding, then, that life is life forevermore, only at ever increasing levels of universal life; that all things begin together and go on together; and that atom, molecule or mass are just the same substance at different rates of vibration, we can see that man is man because he has brought together in form the atoms and molecules fitted to move at the rate of vibration called *human*.

We find ourselves in a world of action in which we have no guide except the date of our coming in. There is one conclusive proof of our rightful place on the path and that is the day, month and year of our birth. No one can deceive himself or others about this fact. We are born just when we are born, and not a moment before or after. We may not know the date of this contact with sentient life, but the date is fixed all the same in the Cosmic.

AN INITIATION EXAMPLE

H-a-r-r-y G-r-o-v-e-n-o-r

(Born the 1st day of the 2nd month of 1909)

Adding the numbers (1 plus 2) of the day and month, we have 3, which, added to the numbers of the year year (1909 = 1 + 9 + 0 + 9 = 10), (3 + 10 = 13) reduced to a final digit, gives us the initiation number 4. Now if we will read the lesson of the meaning of 4, we will see just what Harry Grovenor has coming to him in life; whether he takes his initiations well or ill depends on how well he understands life. His initiation is 4 made of 13, which is a special number vibration.

When we study the meanings of numbers, with their negative and positive sides, we find there is no such thing as fate, that fate is only the things we draw to ourselves by our own birth, and destiny is simply living up to the big vibrations which are within us.

All initiations are big tests, and everyone must learn slow self-conquest and comradeship with the things in his life which cause him to be big.

If we want recognition in anything we have to do the things necessary to get it. If we want wealth we must stimulate our wealth vibrations. In order to get bigger things we must put the balance of our consciousness on the side of our strongest vibrations. This will attract to us on our path the people and things which will help us in that way.

We all have vibrations which, if cashed in, would bring us a million dollars; but before we can get a million dollars, we must give its value in exchange. The thing we want and our point of attraction must be equal.

No one need think he has too hard a task to meet his initiation. At most, life only hands us "9" initiations, and, although we may fail again and again, we will meet it until we have mastered it. Sometimes we get a passing grade and can go on into some new vibration; but we go conditioned, like a student passing into a higher grade in school, who is conditioned in grammar or arithmetic. While we study the next lesson we have to make up the grade behind us.

There are many people who have many grades not quite finished, and who are conditioned in more than one thing. These have the same numbers over and over again in their names, as, for example, *Johnson Woodward Woolsey*. Here is o six times. As o is 6, and the meaning of 6 is domesticity and respectability, it is plain that Johnson has not yet learned this lesson, as all these numbers are his soul numbers. So, someday, somewhere, no matter how much time he takes nor how long he goes on conditioned, Johnson will have to learn how to express for himself and others a holy home. And, he will get 6 as an initiation number until he has included its meaning.

The reason so many are striving and never getting on in life is often revealed by these conditioned grades. They are balancing their books of actions in this life; they are learning the initiations they have failed to learn before.

When we know what our initiation is, we have only to build the essence of it into our character, and meet constructively the experiences which this initiation demands.

The nine initiations can be classified as follows:

1. Individuality
2. Association
3. Expression
4. Organization
5. Freedom
6. Domesticity
7. Aloneness
8. Power
9. Love—Compassion

All double symbols, it must be remembered, are just some more of the same thing. They mean the spiritual, as well as the material initiation, bringing the soul into the consciousness of the whole—the outside and the inside clue.

Our initiation, made up of number-vibrations of day, month and year of our birth, shows us the kind of people, situation and things which will bring us experience in life. "Tell me with whom you associate and I'll tell you what you are," is a true statement. Our initiation may be our fate number, and not one jot or tittle of the law will pass away. Cultural equality is the only open door, and living up to the biggest things in our initiation vibration is our soul's true growth.

AN INITIATION EXAMPLE

Day	Month	Year
1	2	1909 = 4

Why do we take the day first, the month second, and the year last, to find the initiation number? Simply because it is the Cosmic Law. All time is measured by seconds, minutes, hours, days, weeks, months, years, and we cannot withdraw from this cosmic rhythm and keep the true pace.

So we first set the number vibrations of the day (which contains all the vibrations of the seconds and minutes), then the month vibration, and then the year. After we have reduced both the day and the month numbers to a single digit each, we reduce their sum also to a single digit, add to this the digit of the year, and again reduce this sum to a single digit. Then we have the number symbol of the initiation which we will meet, or the number of fate changeless and eternal for this life.

SUMMARY

Summing up the name of Harry Grovenor, we find that his numbers are:

    Personality 4
    Soul 9
    Destiny 4
    Initiation 4

These, with one exception, 9, are all number-symbols of the outside vibrations of life. Harry Grovenor has only two vibrations to live through, so we know that he will not have a very strenuous life if he stays true to the higher laws of his numbers.

We can reasonably expect to find him wealthy, honoured and respected by people because of his soul of 9, secure in his own conceit and surrounded with worldly possessions which delight the 4 mentality.

We also see that he has taken over the vibrations of 4 three times, and this shows us that he has had a hard time learning to live for others and to soften the SELF of 4 into harmonious relationship with humanity. But he has another chance in this life, and if he follows truly the positive side of his present vibrations, we may be sure that he will have name, place, power and authority, and he will be a corner stone on which many will build up their own greatness. The 9 in his soul shows that he has a magnet within which will help him to overcome this selfishness and attract big kindnesses to himself.

The personality, soul, composite self (destiny), and initiation, it must be remembered, are all just simply " states of consciousness " in us which we are continually expressing.

Sometimes these different states of mind clash fiercely, especially if they are composed of *odd* and *even* concords, and they must be harmonized and controlled before we can feel the real pleasure of our own selfhood.

These warring vibrations can be subdued by adding them together and finding their digit, then cultivating the quality of mind which this digit indicates, when we may come to a point of perfect peace where we can live happily with ourselves.

EXAMPLE

Personality	4	(Service—Organization)
Soul	7	(Rest—Silence)
Destiny	5	(Personal Freedom)
	16	=7
Initiation	11	(Religion—Universality)

It can be seen that this example is in great inharmony for the expression of the desires and ambitions of the 11 —there are so many different impulses struggling for completion.

We find that we do not add the 11; it stands for its own spirituality and calls for ideality in all things. The 16 is one of the malefics and means great emotional discontent. Reduced, it digits 7, the path of aloneness and silence. By exercising the silence, introspection, and wisdom of the 7, this combination of personality, soul,

THE EYES OF TRUTH

destiny, and initiation vibrations can be brought to a common denominator, and harmony will follow. This common denominator would be 11 + 7 = 18 = 9, and living the law of the 9 vibration is the method by which peace, power, and plenty may be brought into the life.

We must live close to the centre of *all* our vibrations if we wish to escape reactions. In unity alone will we find peace.

XVII. THE GREAT WITHIN AND THE GREAT WITHOUT

THE INTROVERT, THE EXTROVERT, AND AND THE SUPRAVERT

In the plan of creation, all intelligence is moving in *nine* creative streams and we have found that these streams of action repeat themselves nine times. It is easy to understand, then, that the numbers 1 to 9 and their doubles contain all there IS, WAS or ever WILL BE.

These singles and doubles are intelligence in action and form. They are always combining and dissolving, always in the part and always in solution in the whole. The inside and outside together form the duality of substance. They are the great unknown ingredients which reduce everything to their own kind, dissolving and amalgamating until posterior identity is lost, yet never loses its identity because it is always coming forth in some new familiar form.

No matter how many times this eternal intelligence disappears and reforms, it never interferes with the original substance. This cannot be added to, nor taken away. Like the glass in a kaleidoscope, we rearrange the patterns, but the glass itself is always the same.

If we want to find the very secrets of creation, we must divide all numbers into the great creative energy of the outside, the extrovert and the great receptive energy of the inside, the introvert, with the combination of the two-in-one, the supravert, always together flinging themselves on, from atom to celestial hosts, persisting and perfecting in endeavour, building and destroying that they may build again. So sure, so definite in creation and destruction are the great creative and receptive energies that they can shape and reshape worlds in space; yet, in the silences of the canyon, they leave not a flower imperfect.

Every man has within himself, as the mould of being, the action of these creative and receptive forces. He is the dual one, and his whole character—his thinking, acting, speaking and being—will correspond with the vibrations which are the most positive. If our name and place in the scheme of things have a majority of the Great Receptive numbers of the *Within*, we will work from the centre of all action outwards. If we have a preponderance of the Great Creative numbers, we will work from the *Without* inwards. When the numbers of the Within and the Without are equal, we become the Duality, or the Supravert.

XVIII. THE GREAT WITHIN

THE INTROVERT

The vibrations of the Great Within are 1, 3, 5, 7, 9, and 33, 55, 77, 99. These are the heart of life, or the bodies of the Great Receptive Cosmic Energy. In full force, they produce transcendental consciousness.

These are the numbers of extended vision—the numbers of the mystic, the prophet and the seer. They are radicals and combine with everything loosely. A man or woman with many introvert numbers is not likely to be considered too faithful to human attachments.

Radical number vibrations mean action without effort —too earnest to be eager. The people of these vibrations can wait; time is the soil in which their souls grow great. They feel that the things of the *Without* will call them and force them out when the time comes and they do not care to hurry. They like quiet, repose and silence. They love the high mountains, the quiet streams and the still forests. One with these vibrations will always be *in* the world—not *of* it, and always a separatist although he lends his time, energy and money. Some of these vibrations are more malleable than others, as 33 and 55, but when the last word is said, they are in a class by themselves.

Numbers 1, 3, 5, 7, 9, and their doubles are the number-vibrations of femininity and introversion. The feminine vibrations hold together, recreate, regenerate, conceal, dissolve, and keep all these qualities of consciousness subjective.

XIX. THE GREAT WITHOUT

THE EXTROVERT, THE SUPRAVERT

THE number vibrations of 2, 4, 6, 8, and 22, 44, 66, 88 are the symbols of the *Great Without*. Their path is through the noise and confusion of life. They are always reducing things to their own substance—compelling, controlling, arranging, throwing down, and building up. They are the Great Adjustors—fixing, mending, and placing things, situations and people.

These vibrations represent the strong, creative, constructive intelligence in action everywhere. With this creative, positive energy all things come into form. " Darkness and silence was on the face of the earth," it is said; the brooding force of the inner substance was there and then God said, " Let there be light," and this great creative energy acting positively without, the universe of form sprang into being.

People with these vibrations never render themselves receptive unless it is to their own advantage, and by so doing they can obtain more dominion and power. They use all life and compel all their circumstances to obey. They will turn naturally from the peace and quiet of the inner life to welcome the friction and the conquest of the outer things. Silence tires them just as effectually as noise bores people of the inner life.

Numbers 2, 4, 6, 8, and their doubles 22, 44, 66, 88, are the number of symbols of masculinity. This force creates, tears down, rebuilds, and then gives all things back to femininity—to the inner side—so that it may conceive anew and bring forth on a higher level of life and form.

The outer vibrations are closely combined; they steadfastly hold the force that creates, and always pass quickly into new forms whatever they re-arrange. They are the outside vibrations of the Tree of Life. They may pass from bud to bloom, and from full blossoming through every grade of ripening fruit to the wholly ripened fruit on their tree, but not until they are almost over-ripe do they release and give way to the inner forces which always triumph eventually, for it is written, " Unless a seed die it cannot be born again."

THE TWO BROTHERS
2-4-6-8   1-3-5-7-9

Here is an old mystical story that was told in the past to explain the real meaning of the *Within* and the *Without*.

A father had two sons, *one* who loved silence and dreaming and *one* who loved action and life. Fearing his own ability to direct them, this father called his sons togther and said, " I shall divide my fortune between you and each can take his share and go out into the world and follow his own will. He shall allow himself the privilege of following his own desires and no one shall direct or control. At the end of fifteen years you must both return here; and, if I am alive, you can tell me what you have done with your fortunes and what use you have made of your lives. If I am no longer here to greet you, then you must tell each other and carefully determine which has made the best investment of his time, energy, genius and money."

So the sons received their dowry and the one whose vibrations were most positive in the numbers 2, 4, 6, 8

THE EYES OF TRUTH

and their doubles, decided to remain right where he was and work out his fortune in his own way.

The other son whose vibrations were most positive in 1, 3, 5, 7, 9 and their doubles, left home and went directly to India.

The fifteen years passed and the brothers met as had been agreed. The father had died in the meantime, and so they told each other of their experiences.

The brother who had stayed at home pointed with pride to his possessions. Factories lined the banks of the river; three small towns were built within easy reach on the vacant spots of fifteen years ago; ferry boats ploughed across from town to town and from factory to factory; and fine houses, parks and shining boulevards met the eye wherever it turned. This brother said, " Look! This is what I have done with my money. It tells its own story. This is what I have done, and what I can do as long as I live. Now tell me, what can you do? "

The 1-3-5-7-9 brother thought awhile, then he said, " I can walk on the water." The 2-4-6-8 brother laughed loudly, saying, " Well, all right. Go ahead—let's see you walk." The mystical brother gathered together within himself all the deep occult forces of his being over which he had learned to have control; and, rising into the transcendental place in his own mind, he walked across the river and back. When he finished and stood silent, the other brother only laughed the more loudly and said,

" Is that all you can do? Fifteen years of time, energy and fortune wasted, and all you can do is to walk on the water. After all, you have saved only a penny—that is all it costs to ride—and you have paid out all your fortune just to learn to walk across."

Ridicule and scorn was all he felt for the great mystic who had given his all to find the latent forces dwelling within everyone of us.

This is something like the positions of the inner and outer minds of the present day. Until we understand that life never blunders and that everything is in its rightful place, we will try to force things and people. This is the reason that there are round pegs in square holes and *vice versa.*

It is of the utmost importance that we should know where we belong on the Path of Life, for the things of the outside are not easily found by the inner travellers. It is only through a perfect union within ourselves of our inner and outer forces, that we can win one hundred per cent.

We do not try to live on both sides at once, but remain on our own side while we connect consciously with the natural things of the other side. We must have a body for our thoughts, feelings and purposes. We remain on the outer side if that is our place, and while we are positive in all that the outer means, we do not forget that our body needs a soul, and, that in order to win, we must turn consciously inward in finer and finer selection until we stand perfect—body, mind, soul and spirit.

The numbers of our names and initiations will tell us the truth. " Know the Truth, and the Truth will set you free," is as useful to-day as it was in the beginning.

EXAMPLE

```
A B R A H A M   L I N C O L N
1 2 9 1 8 1 4   3 9 5 3 6 3 5
```

As may be seen, this name has ten inside vibrations and four outside vibrations, forming the vibrations of a true introvert.

THE EYES OF TRUTH

We take as another example the name:

K E I T H   H A M M O T H
2 5 9 2 8   8 1 4 4 6 2 8

Here there are three inside vibrations and nine outside vibrations, forming the vibrations of a true extrovert.

The 1-3-5-7-9 people are a law unto themselves. They begin and stop at their own will. They are on the paths of wisdom, and when fully developed, are out to the land of the naked vision and the single eye.

This does not mean that these states of mind and action are not found to exist in the vibrations of the outside. Not at all. The outside vibrations contain all of these, but they are not positive in *this* side of life; they are concerned mostly with the things of their own vibrations and are positive in these, while the 1-3-5-7-9 or inside vibrations are negative to these outer things and positive to the inward things which are the breath of their lives.

Ideality, love, justice, and humanity are the watchwords of the inner numbers, while to the outer numbers power, name, fame, position and construction represent the ideal. However, it must be remembered that the fully developed life includes the constructive action of both the Within and Without.

THE SUPRAVERT

The duality is the real Supravert or one who has power in both the Within and the Without. He is bound to lean to one or the other, and his real leaning or emphasis is gauged by the numbers in his soul vibration, for we have learned that where the heart is, there will our treasures be.

A true supravert can dominate while he meditates. He has the power of both silence and action, and his pauses are often more dangerous than another's noise and action. Like the storm when it holds its breath in its fury, the supravert can retire into his own consciousness and gather from within a power that neither the true extrovert nor introvert ever touches. And when he brings this force to bear upon any external condition, place or person, he naturally moulds them to his will. He is the master mind—the superman—in any situation.

The supravert vibrations are all double numbers containing an outside and an inside number. When making the balance of numbers in a name, be sure to first take count of the outside and inside numbers, then watch carefully the reduction numbers, also the digits, in order to find out whether the reductions and totals aid the extrovert or introvert side.*

---

* NOTE.—It may be confusing to some to find 1 classified as an introvert number, because of its novitiate creativity and its dominion and power with ability to lead. However, it must be remembered that 1 is a duality and has within itself the unseparated force which it separates at will. When the 1 vibration is rightly understood, we find that all its power comes from its own inborn sense of possessing something which it knows it can depend upon, and not from any visible point of power. This is why the 1 so often seems to be a braggart and a bluffer—he always makes a play of being able to put over the big things which he finally accomplishes.

XX. THE GREAT LAW OF PERIODICITY

CYCLES

A CYCLE is the return of similar vibrations at the pulse beat of time—a day, a week, a month, or a year. Each time a cycle returns it brings an intensified force and with it a larger opportunity and privilege. That is why it is said, " Opportunity only knocks once at every door." However, this is only true in the sense that it comes only once in the same *form*. It will come again and again on the crest of some new impulse, and, at any of these points, if we are ready, we can take advantage of it. If we do not, we only go more and more deeply into debt to life.

The ordinary cycles are 1, 2, 3, 4, 5, 6, 7, 8 and 9. The numbers 10, 11, 22 and the rest of the doubles have no relationship with the ordinary cycles. They represent particular grades in unfoldment, such as certain students in universities take outside of the regular course. Not everyone has these vibrations to contact in their name or birth numbers, but when one does, it is well to remember that 10 is the perfecting vibration, that we have finished our individuality *plus,* have balanced our books and are ready to go on into the next cycle of 11.

Eleven is the balance point between the old cycle and the new. In it one can easily go back to the old habits, the old things of bondage and limitation, or go or into the new power of the new cycle, unencumbered.

Eleven, when lived inharmoniously, is called the path of the penitent. When this grade is made it links with the highest of cosmic cycles, but it always carries with it

WESTERN SYMBOLOGY

the challenge, " Let him that standeth take heed lest he fall."

There are well-known cycles in which we find great opportunities. These are the Power Cycles. The number symbols of the Power Cycles are 3, 5, 7 and 9, and each of these brings us opportunities through the things which they express. Anything that comes back to us on the cycle of 3 we can only secure through the law of 3 which is activity and expression. The cycle of 5 brings its opportunity through the law of freedom and change. In the cycle of 7 we achieve through silence and meditation. In the cycle of 9 we achieve through love and co-operation.

When we meet the cycles of the *double* numbers, we know that we are in the finals of experience and opportunity of their vibrations. The doubles 33, 55, 66, and 99 mean a great deal to us and carry important opportunities. All the other cycles are only the first days in the schoolroom; in them we are only getting ready to pass the final grades, but 22, 33, 55, 77, and 99 are finishing opportunities.

Cycles always intensify as they double in numerical value. In 22 we have twice what we had in 2. In 33 we have three times the advantages we had before. In 44 we have four times the toll to take and pay, and when we come to 99, it is the full measure of the man, and if paid in full, should mean the " Great Conqueror."

Number 66 is called the " House of Last Resorts," for at this point we should have ceased from all efforts and life should bring us all its greatest gifts. Number 66 is called " Heaven and Earth of the Bridal Chamber," and here we can dwell in the place of our own choosing.

Cyclic dates can be found in everything, but we can look to the balancing of life's books in the cycles of 3, 5,

THE EYES OF TRUTH

7, and 9. When we find these vibrations manifesting, we know that they are bringing adjustment of our inner consciousness, and spiritual balance.

Numbers 2, 4, 6, and 8 are great material balance sheets; they clean up our minds and environments.

When our initiation number (of day, month and year) is found, it will always be in one or the other of these cycles. If it is in a single number, we feel that we are in the primaries of the things these numbers mean, but if it totals to one of the double numbers, we know that we are taking a postgraduate initiation, and will learn the experiences of the inner life as well as those of the outer.

The special meanings of the double numbers are:

11. Man and God
22. The world and heaven
33. The flesh and Spirit.
44. Worldly and spiritual organization
55. The world, the flesh, and the Devil, with God, Spirit and Christness
66. The earthly mountain peaks of interior illumination
77. The peace that passeth understanding
88. Material power, with celestial potencies
99. Human love with superhuman compassion

Both sides of life are in these double cycles, and we can choose, this day, which we will serve.

Old age has been called a tragedy, but it is only a tragedy to those who have spent their all in riotous living and arrive at the double-number cycles sterile in activity. We can understand the desolation of age when we see its great opportunities and find that nothing has been gathered into form, no shelter made for a defenceless head, no gifts obtained from life, simply because we used our pearls like gems on a beggar's hand.

Each well-born experience is a step towards God, and the comfort of love and the happiness of life are the gifts which age carries in its hands for those who have lived wisely and well. " Once I was young and now I am old, but never have I seen the righteous or his seed begging bread."

HOW TO FIND OUR PERSONAL CYCLE

To find the personal cycle, take the day, month and year of your birth and reduce them the same as in finding the initiation number. The final digit of this sum will be the cycle vibration under which we will register. Every person is " a law unto himself " under his own particular cycle number.

A PERSONAL CYCLE EXAMPLE

Day Month Year
 1   7   1927 (1 + 9 + 2 + 7 = 19 = 10) = 1
1 plus 7 plus 1 equals 9.

This shows that the person will be under the cyclic vibration of 9, so he can look for his experiences, precipitates and balancing forces in any day, month or year, person, place, or thing, in which the vibration of 9 occurs. This rule holds good for *all* vibrations from 1 to 9 inclusive.

The 5 cycle returns and 5 is found again at 10, 15, 20, 25, 30, 35, 40, 45, 50, the final or double cycle being 55, in which perfect personal and universal freedom should be found.

Following 7, we find that the cycle returns again at 14, 21, 28, 35, 42, 49, 56, 63, 70, with 77 the dual number and final expression of personal and universal

THE EYES OF TRUTH

silence. The spirit of the universe and the spirit of man should be consciously united at this point.

Following on, the cycle of 9 returns again at 18, 27, 36, 45, 54, 63, 72, 81, 90, and 99, which is the full measure of the man, paid in full through accumulated experiences and expression. Those who are in double numbers find that their cycles are farther apart than those in the single numbers.

It must be remembered that cycles identify themselves with people, places, and dates. We must guard all our lines of contact and protect them by putting the full weight of our consciousness and actions *en rapport* with the vibrations of the cycle.

If our cycle is 3, we plunge into expression. Thirty-three is the great final cycle of 3, and here perfect soul expression should be accomplished. If it is 5, we let go of old things; we arrange our life and turn to the new in expectation and power. If it is 7, we withdraw into the silence; if it is 9, we mingle more compassionately with humanity. This is the instruction for all cyclic numbers. If the cycle is a dual number, we must try to combine in harmonious ways both the outer and inner things of the cycle.

By precipitates we mean that at certain times—either days, months or years—we meet the full reactions of our own actions. " All things come home at eventide," " Chickens always come home to roost," " A bad penny always comes back,"—these are wise sayings. They are precipitates of our own life. We must meet ourselves coming and going, and all debts to life must be paid somewhere. In the long run, all love is paid with love, all hate with hate, all loss with more loss, and all gain with more gain. If we have sowed to the wind, we reap the whirlwind of rearrangement, and get back some of the things we have given. If we have sown to love and peace and good, we get these all back. So a cyclic number may bring us great good, and we may find in it a new freedom, but it always brings forth its own kind.

The year 1926 was the end of a cycle (9). The year 1927 digits 10, the new cycle, or the transition number —everything being in process of becoming, with no real stability. The year 1928 digits 11 or 2, the balancing number, in which all the nations will square themselves with one another. And in 1929, which digits 3, they will begin to come on again in more harmonious expression, personal to a great degree, but finer, and they will be more likely to reach an international agreement which will be for the greatest good of each nation. In 1930, which digits 4, we can look for international agreement, organization and dictatorship, from four great powers. In 1931, which digits 5, we will see the agitation of the moral questions, marriage, divorce, motherhood, parentage, and social and religious interpretations. In 1932, which digits 6, we will see a settling down of every nation to the concerns of home, country and national ideals; a closer international family relationship will come—a brotherhood of men which will be the advance guard of an entirely new civilization. Minute by minute, hour by hour, day by day, we record our own selfhood into the eternal life of the universe. From what we call the smallest to the biggest things in our life, there is one long film of registration.

SUMMARY

We carry through with us from year to year the essence of the one great impulse which makes an impression above all others during the year. Many impressions will fade and disintegrate, but the one which remains paramount will go forward with us and cast itself again as the fulcrum from which our whole next year will move into form. This impulse begins when reason begins, and only ends with our closing life.

When this basic impulse is one that has put us ahead and made us more than we were, we find that the new cycle will bring us into contact with the people, places, and things, which help our advancement, and our cycle will be easy, or what the world calls " lucky."

When this one central impression is one of pain, struggling limitations, hard luck, or bitterness, and this impulse colours all the major part of our days, we can be sure that these things will posit as basic principles for our next move, and we will meet the things, persons, places, and experiences which hinder our progress and delay our desires, and we will find ourselves passing through an unsatisfactory development, or what the world calls " bad luck."

Elsewhere, we have learned that these good things or bad things will take on in either cycle the colour and expression of the vibrations of our own individual cycle. If we study the positive and negative meanings of the numbers, we can easily tell what we need to accentuate to aid or delay our precipitates.

There is always the universal cyclic vibration with which our own must coincide, either by natural vibratory relationships or by an induced state of mind which forces the personal into harmony with the universal.

EXAMPLE

Should our personal cyclic vibration, for example, 8 (day, month and year), coincide with the vibration of the immediate year, then we will find a whole year of nonresistance and a subtle co-operation of the things of life which will make it easy for us to realize our ambitions. We will be under the law of similars in vibrations, and this is the holy matrimony or mystical marriage.

Should our cyclic number be in the law of vibrations of opposites (like 4 and 5), or any of the opposite concords, then we will know that we have posited for our basic principle of the year, the lines of action which are not in accord with the universal. We will be obliged, at least, to reduce them to the vibration of complementaries, or we will have a hard year of struggling for conquest under the law of opposition.

Cycles are simply the old idea of fate and destiny explained by number symbols. When we fully understand the vibratory key of life, we find there is no such thing as fate, that it is only the registration of our own negative thinking, speaking and acting brought back to us through limitation of health, success or happiness. And, that destiny is simply the registration of our own fine high thinking and acting which is also brought back to us through people, situations and things which crown our life with health, happiness and prosperity. Whether the law of our cycles shall make us a child of destiny or a victim of fate, is in our own hands.

BOOK TWO
The Love Story of the World

BOOK TWO

THE LOVE STORY OF THE WORLD

XXI. LOVE, MARRIAGE, DIVORCE

IN order to understand the importance of the vital subjects of marriage, love, and divorce, we must take the original nine vibrations, 1 to 9, inclusive, and divide them into concords—the odd and the even.

The numbers of the even concord are 2, 4, 6, 8, 22, 44, 66, and 88. The numbers of the odd concord are 1, 3, 5, 7, 9, 11, 33, 55, 77, and 99.

The two concords run through every expression of life. They are found in body, mind, soul, and spirit. In all things, through all things, we must contact all life in one or both concords, or in mixture of each.

These two streams of intelligence in action are always combining to make the perfect whole. They combine in three different contacts which determine the law operating in persons, places, or things.

The three combinations are the similars, opposites, and complementaries. The similars are the numbers of the same concord, as 3 and 3, 5 and 5, 7 and 7, 2 and 2, 4 and 4, 8 and 8 and 9 and 9. Opposites are combinations of inside and outside numbers, such as 2 and 3, 3 and 4, 4 and 5, 5 and 6, 6 and 7, 7 and 8, and 8 and 9. Complementaries are combinations of different numbers of the same concord—all odd or all even—as 2, 6, and 8, or 3, 5, and 7.

The number is always a symbol of qualities of consciousness. We know that when one is a certain num-

WESTERN SYMBOLOGY

ber at soul he will always be the thing his symbol indicates,—6 at soul will always be 6, and 5 will always be 5,—it is the very colour of their lives, and nothing will ever make them change completely.

There will be grades and grades of the soul number. It may be composed of different vibrations, but, in the last analysis, it will be what it is. For instance, there may be one 6 made up of 5 and 1, and another 6 made up of 4 and 2, but both 6's will express the qualities of 6. However, 4 will not be like 5, and 7 will never be like 8, no matter how they may sum up their vibrations. Number 8 made up of 4 and 4 will find likes in common with 7 made up of 3 and 4, but 8 will never find true harmony with 7.

XXII. COMBINATIONS FOR TRUE LOVE AND HAPPY MARRIAGE

The combinations of similars are the ones for happy marriages and happy love stories. Every marriage or love experience in the world is the RIGHT marriage and RIGHT love, but only now and then do we find the TRUE marriage and the TRUE love.

All marriages, or love experiences, outside of the true combinations are initiations in which we learn the next lessons we have set for our own soul.

The TRUE marriage claims all and gives all. " All mated—body, mind, soul and spirit." Being for being in perfect part, life for a life, soul for a soul, heart for a faithful heart.

Not all marriages are made in the laws that bring happiness; not all love stories are lasting, because it is not a part of the Great Eternal Plan that they should be. We must meet ourselves at every turn of the wheel of life, and the SELF has many extensions of experiences.

When we meet ourselves in form we must take the consequences of our own desires. We must know that we do meet in form every desire of our life that we have intensified enough to pass into form. " The thing thou cravest so, waits in the distance, wrapped in the silences, unseen and dumb."

" Desire is the prophecy of its fulfillment," and it is always fulfilled for us by people, situations, or things. We gather at our harvest what we sow. If we have sown hate, we get hate back again in some form. All our negative states are embodied just as surely as our positive ones. Love and hate are twin-born, and it only

WESTERN SYMBOLOGY

takes a strengthening of the vibration of either to bring them into form.

The Ancients said, "In some incarnation we have to marry the Devil." When we can live with him, he leaves us and we are free forever.

When we remember that the "Devil" is only someone who has in himself all those negative states of consciousness we have had, or have, which we have not transmuted, we can easily see how we may attract to ourselves certain persons, situations or things which will test us until we learn to include them.

So it is not hard to understand a RIGHT marriage. The person we marry is just the law bringing us our own, and not one jot or tittle of the law will pass away until we fulfill it—and love is the true fulfillment of the law.

None of the great world work is ever done by the TRUE lovers. (They are too satisfied.) They find each other, and life has nothing else that they want. They live for each other and for each other's desires. They work together—there is only one world for them and just two people in it. Their children rise up and call them blessed, but the great struggling world rarely hears of them or of their deeds.

For those who truly love, life runs on like a song. Love must love, that is all it has to do and it keeps steadily at its work. For two who love, there is rest and peace; and they do not have time or inclination to talk or write about it. "From the heart of the man who was homeless came the deathless song of home, and the praises of rest are chanted best by those who are forced to roam." Always it is so,—"The heart once filled, the voice is stilled, and we stand in the silence dumb."

THE LOVE STORY OF THE WORLD

"Where your heart is, there will your treasure be also." And if we look for perfect harmony, satisfaction, and rest, we must find out where our heart is, and who is walking through the pathway of life with us.

When the heart is filled, there is nothing more to say about it. Love just loves, and all life is satisfactory. Living in the One Life, in the One Mind, the One Body, the One Soul, there is nothing we lack or miss.

The digits of the soul-numbers and the initiation-numbers must be similar. This is the true symbol of affinities—and harmony is their birthright.

EXAMPLE

John Ryan Croydel —born 1st day of the 8th month,
  6   1   6 5   year 1889

Elsa May Bowen   —born 7th day of the 2nd month,
 5 1   1   6 5   year 1889

Adding the vowel numbers of Elsa May Bowen we find the digits are 7 and 11 in the soul vibrations.

Adding the vowel numbers of John Ryan Croydel, we find the digits of his soul vibrations are also 7 and 11.

Adding the day and month of Elsa's initiation, reduced to a single digit, to the final vibration of her year, we have 8. Then taking the digit of the day and month of John's initiation and adding it to the digit of his year, we have 8 also.

This shows us that at soul or in the very centre of their beings they love the same things—are one with the same substances of life, and when we turn to the iniations we find them together in the same class, studying the same things, and learning the same experiences in the same way.

They will find complete and perfect happiness, for " it is love that makes the world go round " and lends a glamour to all activities. So we know that earth has no sorrow that will divide or mar the lives of Elsa and John. They are taking the same lessons, they pass the same examinations, there is no longer any quest—each has found the Other Self. The two are one in ideals and action. They can walk on, hand in hand, can be sure that there is a love that reaches to the edge of the grave and on beyond into the dreams to come.

It is part of the soul's great need to have a confessional. Only those who love us can give us peace or truly comfort us. Only those can perfectly comfort us who come naturally into our being, not in correction, but in sweet unchiding understanding—those who have the same substance in their being which we have in ours.

XXIII. MARRIAGE FAILURES

Is marriage a failure? This is the age-old question, and the answer is *no*. Marriage is only a failure for those to whom it is a failure. There are thousands of marriages which are not failures, but the world never hears of them. It is the *failure* marriage that keeps all the headlines in the papers, and to which humanity is always directing its attention.

LOVE is eternal. Holy matrimony began when the ONE was made TWO, and this union is eternal and indestructible. " What God has joined together, no one can put asunder."

We do not find perfect love in every incarnation. We have many different levels of life to include, and many experiences to pass through as we go on in our larger self-expression, and only when, within our own being we have the active vibrations of a true, divine love, can we be sure that there will come to us the outside picture of our own perfected self. When we have the vortex of divine loving in our soul, then we may be sure we will kiss the lips of our desire.

Until then, we grow through our experiences of loving in the part—not in the whole. If we sin against love in any way, we set the law of our own correction; and we will pay in full, no matter how much we hope to escape it. Markham says,
" One thing shines clear in the world's mad reason,
   One lightning over the chasm runs—
That to turn from LOVE is the world's one treason,
   And treads down all the Suns."

XXIV. CAUSES OF UNHAPPY MARRIAGES

THE LAW OF OPPOSITES

The cause of unhappy marriages is found in the mating of opposites in soul consciousness and in initiations. The educators of olden times taught falsely that the law of opposites was the basis of happy marriages. This is one of the great misleading instructions of to-day; and, yet, at its root, lies the germ of truth. The falsehood can be cleared away only by the light of higher revelation and explanation.

The law of opposites holds good only as far as the physical body is concerned. Nature hates a tangent, and will never let anything go too far in any one direction. So a tall man marries a short woman and the children return to normal height. A blonde marries a brunette, and a medium colour results. This attraction is the primitive impulse of nature that must keep everything normal, and which always acts where it is needed to balance forces; but it has no power save on the physical plane, and it is not the law of attraction by which men and women find their very own.

We can prove this very quickly, because everyone knows how soon physical attractions die out, or cool, and how often it has been found that in their passing nothing else remains. The marriage is a dead thing, and the husband or wife find themselves tied for life to the dead body of a worn-out desire.

When we are entirely opposite in soul and initiation

vibrations, there is little hope for perfect peace and harmony. We can learn the lesson our association holds for us, and do our best, but nothing can deceive the heart into believing that it has been fully satisfied.

The law of opposites is of value in business psychology. In that division we will review it again. In love and marriage its power ends with the physical or personality vibrations, and we must leave it there or suffer.

XXV. TYPES OF INHARMONY

THERE are many types of inharmony—many people bound together in this life, fighting through, struggling, perhaps sometimes enduring, yet never knowing why, and never learning the method of living life in a bigger way.

The divorce courts are full of these cases. Humanity only judges, then condemns, while everywhere are the wrecks of great lives and noble hearts who tried with all their might, yet failed to get on. They might have lived in harmony together had they known some system by which they could have found a common point of of action.

Those who have 6 as a soul number can look for great *inharmony* with those who have 5 as a soul number. If they have these opposites in the initiations, it is also perilous. The 6 person is domestic and home-loving, fond of children, friends, respectability and responsibility, and is devoted; all that makes for publicity is naturally distasteful to it. It loves home life, protection, food and a few people. It shirks notoriety in any form, and the Many is less precious to it than the *One*.

Number 6 is the conventional vibration while 5 is the unconventional. Number 6 is strong on virtue, and 5, although virtuous, is light on application, careless in precepts, and inclined to mind its own business and let the world alone. This often infuriates the mother-minded 6. The 5 is a natural sport, loves everything light and entertaining, while 6 is a home lover, quiet and steadfast.

THE LOVE STORY OF THE WORLD

When these vibrations meet, love, or marry under the law of attraction of opposites, they will have to know a higher law than the ordinary married couples know, or they will drift into inharmony that is never healed because it reaches to the fundamentals of their lives.

Numbers 8 and 7 bring discord when they are married or even come together in a love story. Number 7 is the number of silence and meditation; 7 loves the silent things of life and dreads publicity and notoriety, while 8 is proud of his name, power and position, and, when he has secured these, he rejoices in living up to them.

The 8 loves noise and outside show. The 7 loves softness, quiet, and a simple life. Sometimes an 8-power man drags a soft, silent, 7 wife with him through all of his notoriety and public life; and, when she becomes ill, he spends many dollars on doctor's bills to make her well, never thinking that if he would give her a chance to retreat and retire from external vibrations of people and things, she would get strong and fine through the healing currents within her own being.

Numbers 1 and 2, and 3 and 4 are all opposites. When these meet and marry, they find they differ in the very soul of things. When their initiations are opposite it is not strange to find them drift apart, each being filled with different interests which different people minister to their lives.

When we remember that all marriages are RIGHT marriages and only a few are TRUE marriages, we can understand that all these marriages and loves in the law of opposites are simply lessons we have taken on to include. All RIGHT marriages are, therefore, of

101

importance, and it is very essential that we know just what lesson we have to learn from each other.

EXAMPLE

James Perks —born 2nd day of the 3rd month, year 1883

Jenny Bronson—born 5th day of the 1st month, year 1885

It will be seen that James Perks is " 11 " in soul and 7 in initiation. He must take the experiences of 7. We know by this that he is bound to be interested in things of the interior—a true introvert, while his initiation will incline him to turn to the idealistic and religious.

Since Jenny Bronson is an 8 made up of 5 and 3, we know that her soul is fixed on material things; she is a lover of form and outer expression—a true extrovert. Interpreting these vibrations, we find exactly what she would be under the law of opposites with James Perks. Her ideality of soul and purpose will be entirely different from his. Inasmuch as she would have 6 and 22 as her initiation, her lesson is power through notoriety and the public side. We can easily understand that these two might find things very unsatisfactory.

It does not take long to discover just what sort of life they would lead together. He will be just what his soul qualities declare him to be. She will be true to her own qualities, because it is a part of the divine plan that we shall not lose our own individualities. But this will not make for harmony between them. Only when they learn to study the lesson which the other one has for them, can they find peace. James must learn how to link himself up occasionally with some of the outer gaieties of the world. Jenny must learn to come away

THE LOVE STORY OF THE WORLD

from the outer world some of the time and find the deeps of silence and inner self-realisation.

The 11 and 22, or the double vibrations, open another fertile field for inharmony. The 22 admires the ideality of 11, and 11 admires the power and strength of 22, so the marriage is consummated. Then the test begins. The 11 finds that all the splendid physical strength which he admired in 22 is gained by methods of living in which he can have little part. She has methods of expression with which he is totally unfamiliar. She finds that he is a creature of another world, and that the beauty and illumination which fascinated her thrives on things which he cannot give.

The 11 finds that 22 lives in a natural universe, in a natural body, and with natural habits. She does not know that the soul within him longs and hungers for things sublime. She only knows that she wants her dinner, plenty of it, and on time, while she finds that he wants silence and that her ideals of food, sex, and associations in general are so attenuated that he can find little satisfaction in them.

After a while they naturally come to the parting of the ways. The 22 goes to a lawyer and calls 11 a freak. In turn, 11 calls 22 a brute. Both are right and both are wrong. Number 22 would not be a brute to a woman whose soul was filled with the desires of 22; and 11 would not be a freak to a man who had the soul longings of an 11. They are *misfits* and they do not know that they must learn the lesson which each brings to the other before they can make the perfect ONE.

This is the inevitable outcome of the marriage of opposites. Such marriage failures vary in degree only. The couples do not always find divorce courts—but they find hours of soul-longings for that which they

103

have not, and many hours of soul-discipline. Sometimes they work towards each other in a bigger spirit of giving and taking, but life is never just right or complete.

When persons meet and think that they are in love, it is not likely that a few lessons in numerology will stop them from marrying; nor is it likely that they will listen much to what is said. But those who do listen and understand will find that even though their marriage may be, or is, an initiation marriage, they can learn the reason for all their differences and begin to study the lesson they bring to each other. Thus, through a better understanding, they will find a common denominator for peace.

The only instruction thta can be given to those who are working through an unhappy marriage is to " pal up." We can live with anyone if we think we can. We live with every sort of person as a travelling companion and do not quarrel; so, when those of opposite vibrations are linked up together in marriage, they might just as well try to be pals—and give and take.

It is not hard to live with anyone when we live half the time at our own point of understanding and the other half at theirs. We then learn the lesson they have to teach us, and they learn from us.

We can be *happy* when married to our exact polar opposite if we never forget that it takes all sorts of experiences to make the soul express perfection. The biggest life is the one that includes the most. The perfect life is the one that expresses constructively for himself and others the wisdom he includes.

XXVI. COMPLEMENTARY MARRIAGES

COMPLEMENTARIES, as we have said before, are the numbers of the same concord, 2, 4, 6, and 8, or 1, 3, 5, 7, and 9. The saying is, " friendship is akin to love," and it is. Complementaries constitute the law of friendships and brotherly love; such vibrations give lasting friendliness.

The marriages of these vibrations of complements are cool, dispassionate and comfortable. They never know the misery of doubts and fears. They are never jealous; they love in a friendly, brotherly and sisterly fashion; and no great heights or depths of feeling mark their lives.

In these marriages there is a great deal of respect and admiration for each other. They sometimes go on in this calm stream of undisturbed content for many years, although haunted now and then, perhaps, with the knowledge that life is not quite all that it might be. However, not really knowing what they have missed, they live and die in peace.

But, again and again, these marriages have another ending. They may go on in this undisturbed way until " Mr. Right," or " Miss Right," comes along; and then their peace ends. It is written, " We may mistake a fancy for a passion, but we never mistake a passion for a fancy when it comes." Complementaries will often discover, when it is too late, that they have been living in a fancy.

WESTERN SYMBOLOGY

Sometimes they part and go on their ways, and there is little trouble about it. Whatever may be the events, there is never the struggle, hate and strife that we find in the separation of opposites. Often they go on living their lives out in the same old way, because they know that no one can step over a human heart to happiness. They learn to wait.

Not until those of the marrying world learn to stop, look and listen, will they be forewarned about their marriage ventures. When they do they will find that life, in its wisdom, has hung its signals everywhere, and that he who runs may read.

As humanity rises in consciousness and understanding of the laws of finer selection, it will not rush headlong into agreements which it cannot keep; or which, at best, it will keep unrighteously. In the new civilization marriage will be guarded from the beginning and then there will be no backwash of human unhappiness. Boys and girls will be taught numerology and, by the time they leave the common schools, they will know themselves—know what to undertake as their life's work, and whom to marry. This will end the great grist of unhappy marriages and the divorces which we inherited in the old-world way of hopeless ignorance.

If we ever expect to find happiness, we must find our very own in every contact which we make with life. We may always know our own at every turn of the path of life, for when we find it we will find that in the Soul and Initiation—there is the very counterpart of our SELF—and we can say, " I knew you, somehow, when I met you just now; for you are the ideal of my dreams. I always knew 'twould be someone like *you*. I've loved you forever, it seems."

106

SUMMARY

Remember:

1st, Concords and their divisions.

2nd, Similars, conplementaries, and opposites.

3rd, Similars—the law of happiness.

4th, Opposites—the law of inharmony.

5th, Complementaries—the law of friendship.

6th, Similarity of soul and initiation vibrations imperative for harmony.

7th, Opposites mean initiation marriages—with a lesson to learn.

8th, Understanding of true character is the key to perpetual harmony.

XXVII. THE SECRET IN MARRIAGE NAMES

A WOMAN always assumes the surname of her husband and thereby brings about certain changes in her own number symbols. Does she lose or gain? And, what is the effect of the accumulation of feminine vibrations upon the husband? Does he, too, change? Or are the additional vibrations simply absorbed in his own?

The answer is simple. We never escape our own vibrations; the number symbols in the name given to us constitute our deck of cards with which we play our game of life. We do not lose any of them by marriage; they are only absorbed *in* and manifested *through* the new symbols which we add to those we already had. A woman may be 5 in soul; and, through marriage, she may take on 6 and become an 11. This only means that she will manifest as 5 on a spiritual vibration. Or, she may be a 9 and by marriage become a 1. Basically she will never cease to be a 9, but she will express her 9 consciousness through the opportunities of 1. Thus she becomes a very individualized 9.

No matter to what division of the self a new number symbol is added, it does not take away anything, whether it is a vibration of soul, personality, destiny, or initiation. It only gives a new dress to the same ego —just adds some new cards to the old deck. Mary Brown will still be Mary Brown in any style of dress, in a hovel or in a palace, at work or at rest, alone or in a crowd, rich or poor; but her clothes and situations will give her opportunity for different expressions of her real self. Mary Brown may marry John Smith and be obliged to express her own soul consciousness of 7 through the added consciousness of 9 in the soul of Smith. However, Mary Brown Smith will still be silent, and not quite so genial and comradely as one who was 9 in the beginning.

Clara Burns may be a 5 in soul, and become a 6 in soul consciousness by marriage. While she may express herself domestically and with respectability, she will have a love of sports, change, and pleasure which is not found in the soul of a purely 6 woman.

Men also retain all their vibrations in marriage but their own vibrations are modified to express those of the woman they include. A man with a 7 soul consciousness may add the soul consciousness of a woman of 6, and he will grow to be more domesticated and talkative as the association continues, although he is not basically altered.

As consciousness and individuality in everybody is rising, the men and women of this present-day civilization are more and more seeking to retain their own names. Ten years ago we could travel with just the signature of Mr. and Mrs. Harrison and maid, or valet; but that is not done to-day. The maids and valets insist on an individuality. They are Miss or Mr. as well as their masters. Mrs. Jane Harrison is as important as Mr. Henry Harrison. Restaurant tables of to-day may hold a card reading, " Your waiter is Mr. ——," or " Miss ——," as the case may be. Bank tellers' names are at their windows, and the names of room clerks at hotels are shown on cards placed on their desks.

Women who have attained success and fame in some work before marriage are insisting on keeping their own names and their old business signatures. They do not care to use names which have not helped them to

WESTERN SYMBOLOGY

the top, names which would almost force them to begin all over again. A new name often blankets an old firm. Individuality is at a high valuation and bigger vision brings added power.

In this new age, women belong to themselves, and " Mrs." is slowly being discarded. Grace de Vere would rather have her own name and all the vibrations which have made her great, and write beneath it, if necessary, " wife of Ross Kinsey," than to submerge all her own consciousness and attraction except that which might come to her as " *Mrs. R. Kinsey.*" As soon as the soul expands it naturally seeks more space and larger lines of attraction.

Anyone who has a very long name will do well to select from it the very strongest number symbols which are in line with his desire, and thereby reduce his name to a concentrated contact. His vibrations will then become like a hose with a nozzle and he will have a better opportunity to direct his personal forces.

We have already said that as one rises in power, greatness, recognition and consequence, all superfluous names are dropped. We say Napoleon, Bismarck, Wellington, Grant, Lincoln, Wilson. Greatness never carries baggage. Any power increases as it is compressed and directed.

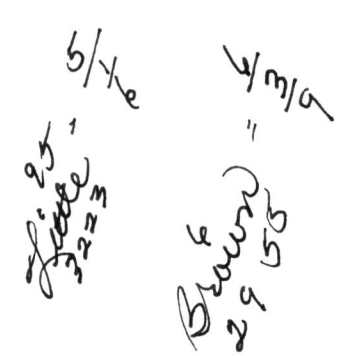

XXVIII. WEDDING DAYS

HOW TO START TOWARD THE THINGS DESIRED

THE wedding month, the wedding day, the wedding hour—these have always been supremely important. The many inharmonious marriages that fill the world are sufficient testimony concerning the ignorance shown in contracting marriages.

June is called the month of marriages and orange blossoms. There are *three* 6's in the soul of orange blossoms; and this does not happen by accident. June is the six month of the year and symbolizes marriage, parenthood, domesticity, respectability, and responsibility. The soul of June is 8, therefore it is the peace and power of home.

Also, speaking mystically, June is the first *free* month. February, March, April, and May are called *bond* months. They never symbolize marriage, although marriages do take place in them. But the true marriage vibrations are found in June. Furthermore, June is a summer month, and the vibration of the soul of summer is $3 + 5 = 8$, while the soul of winter is $9 + 5 = 14 = 5$, the shifting base.

June is mystically called " The Ruler Month " and all its subjects, married or single, have a right to expect conquest, also superiority in some degree. Therefore it is quite natural that June should be the real marriage month, for in the union of two people there is always in both hearts the longing for better things and happier days which the marriage is expected to bring.

Of course, it is well to remember that all months are good months when the unions are true unions. All days are good days, and all years good years; but, notwithstanding this, there *are* months and years which are good, better, or best for each of us individually.

When we choose a wedding day we should choose the day that is in affinity with our desires. Just as there are similars, opposites, and complementaries in marriage, there are the same conditions in wedding days. Those who are contracting should arrange to have the day of the month coincide with their most intensified vibrations.

EXAMPLE

Suppose the soul of the bride is 3 and the soul of the bridegroom is 6. We should find the wedding day vibrations which carry in themselves the soul of both parties of the wedding; for where their hearts are, there will be their treasures. The first choice for their wedding day should be a day with the vibration of 9, or the sum of the soul of the two. Suppose the soul of the bride is 5 and the soul of the bridegroom 7. Adding these two vibrations makes 12, which, reduced to a single digit, is 3. This wedding day will hold in it the soul of the two.

Suppose the soul of one is 6 and the soul of the other is 5. Then the soul of the wedding day will be 11—a *test* wedding day. Number 11 is the hardest of all vibrations because it demands such high standards of living. Any deviation from the level of ideality, honesty, or truth will bring reactions which are hard to overcome. This is why the ancients called it " the Path of the Penitent."

THE LOVE STORY OF THE WORLD

The wedding day vibrations are real and sure, and there is no use in hoping to get something from nothing. If we want the things of 8, we must marry in the 8 vibration; if we want the things of 7, we must marry in the 7 vibration; etc., etc. The meaning of a number and its relation to things tell us the story. On the path of life, like attracts like; men do not gather grapes from thorns nor figs from thistles.

In selecting a wedding day for our own greater accomplishment, it is imperative that we should know just how to combine the vibrations of life so that they can bring to us our hearts' desires.

It is of no profit to combine for silence when we want noise and excitement; nor is it worth while to combine for religious positions when our whole desire is for material place and power.

Possessions in life depend mainly upon our deep soul desires:

The THING thou cravest so, waits in the distance—
   Wrapped in the silences, unseen and dumb,
Essential to your soul and your existence.
   Live worthy of it; call,—*and it must come.*

This is as true as life itself is true. However, we must know how to live worthy of the thing which we crave, and we must know how to call for it in no uncertain tones.

Every vibration in the world either works *for* us or *against* us. We must be strong and self-reliant if we would control all vibrations which work against us and turn them to our own account. Our soul numbers are our true selves, but we may desire some special realization in marriage.

WESTERN SYMBOLOGY

If we want wealth, we must choose material and outside vibrations. If we want power, we must choose power vibrations, and also choose them along the particular line of power which we desire. If we want home, freedom, seclusion, fame, individuality, or any of the things men seek to secure, then we must marry in the vibrations which augment these vibrations in ourselves. (Study carefully the meanings of the numbers.)

Many women love popularity, strength, and position. They like to say " My husband," because it strengthens their own egos and makes them feel more important. To other women the sweetest name on earth is " The father of my children." And again, other women desire fine homes and lovely possessions. Others want friends and the opportunity to live with those who can make them happy.

Some women want all life to be a bridal chamber where incense burns day and night. Some women want life to be a temple where nothing but worship can enter. To these personal association must always be a prayer. They want someone to work with in the world, but in their mate they hope to find the temple of the living God.

It can easily be seen why so many wedding days do not satisfy those who marry. They marry in ignorance and repent in misery. We must know *what* we want and *how* to combine for it; then the days will repeat themselves, in increasing degrees, for our own good.

WEDDING DAYS AND DESIRES

1 = Individual interest and larger mental development

2 = Harmony without effort—attraction

3 = Personal accomplishment and lightness of life—happiness
4 = Material growth and personal accomplishment with others
5 = Freedom, travel, and a chance to change
6 = Parenthood, children, home and protection
7 = Solitary home life—one world with two people in it—separateness
8 = Public life, company, money and material gain
9 = Fellowship, many friends, the chance to help humanity
11 = Spiritual unfoldment, worship, praise and prayer
22 = Outside interests, great enterprise, more world than home—spiritually material.

Remember, the double vibrations are simply cycles of some more of the same thing. They bring the experiences of both outside and inside things—life contains both material and spiritual adventures.

XXIX. WEDDING HOURS

THE *hour* of the wedding day is of equal importance, and it should be chosen to accord with the highest desires of the couple.

High noon has always been one of the hours chosen by mystics. That is 12; and 12, reduced, makes 3, which is a happy vibration for all the world. The number 3 is the symbol of perfected self-expression, and in this vibration each one has an equal chance. At noon the highest vibrations of the day reach the earth. It is always well to touch the best.

The vibration of the daytime is better than the vibration of the night time. The soul of the daytime is 6, which is the marriage vibration. The soul of night time is 5. This is the vibration of the earthly divine, while 6 is the individuality on the domestic cycle.

It is also true that daytime marriages are bound to bring a life of more activity than do those of the night time. There is a daytime force and a night time force. The sun, with broad daylight and daytime force, makes for action, effort and creation. The night and night time force makes for seclusion, rest and obscurity, and for instability and inertia.

It must be remembered that wherever our soul is, there will our treasure be. If we have most of our numbers on the vibrations of the outside daylight force, we must choose a corresponding outside material vibration for a wedding day, or *vice versa*. Some people think that a vibration of one sort of force needs an opposite vibration to balance it. Under all circumstances, this works out to adjustment; but it is the hard law of *opposites*. It is better to add more and more of the same thing until it reaches the center of a true balance, and reaches it in rest and peace and in similarity of purpose,—not through the law of discontent, opposition and struggle.

Some people marry for a home, protection, and children. These should choose 6 or some multiple of 6 for the wedding day.

Some people marry for rest and obscurity, for protection from effort, for soul unfoldment, and for spiritual satisfaction. They should choose the spiritual vibrations for the wedding day.

When we have found just where we are in number vibrations, we will have no trouble selecting a wedding day that may bring everything we desire into the channel of our life. There is nothing to stand in our way when we are one with our own substance in body, mind, soul and spirit. The wedding day can become the tie that binds in kindred fellowship; and, through it, we can be divinely known and expressed.

XXX. MATCHING SYMBOLSCOPES FOR MARRIAGE

To match symbolscopes for marriage, read each name separately; then compare the digits of Personality, Soul, Destiny (or vocation), and Initiation. Be sure to ascertain how the soul, personality, destiny and initiation combine in concords, to know if they are opposites, complementaries, or similars, and remember what these concords mean. The vibrations must be in concord of *soul* and *initiation*. They must be alike in the *soul* digit and in the *initiation* digit before there can be a perfect affinity. The different numbers composing the final digit is sufficient for variety of character.

Personality and destiny may combine as they will. They will be swept along in the stream of harmony which the same soul and the same life initiations bring. There is bound to be happiness when souls and initiations are one—it is some more of the same self.

To know the vibrations a woman assumes when she marries, and to find out whether she gains or loses, we must count the numbers that are alike in both names. Each number lacking in either name symbolizes a lesson to be learned. For instance, a man may not have a 7 in his name, while the woman has more than one 7. This is the thing he takes on with her. In like manner, all the numbers in his name which she does not have are the things she takes on with him. It is of no use to bother about the same numbers, for they are just some more of the same things and will make for harmony between them. The numbers which they have *not*, and which they must learn through each other, are the *tests* they set for themselves in marriage. However, remembering that the biggest life is the life which includes the most, they should just nobly set about learning the lessons which their own desires have brought to them; and, after awhile, they will express perfectly all of the new vibrations.

EXAMPLE

```
M i n n i e   H u n t l e y
4 9 5 5 9 5   8 3 5 2 3 5 7

J o s e p h   B e e r i n g
1 6 1 5 7 8   2 5 5 9 9 5 7
```

Minnie Huntley has no 1 or 6. She will be required to meet these in Joseph Beering, and to get so used to them that she will include them with her own vibrations, if she wants to be a perfect wife. Joseph Beering has no 3 or 4 in his composition. He can know that he will meet these things in Minnie Huntley, and, he will include them before he can make her entirely happy.

When married couples know what they need to do, they can soon meet their experiences in a big way. They will understand that *live and let live* is the true way of love and life. Whenever the numbers they have to include are many, they will not find life together any too easy; but a deep understanding of their mutual need will make the situation full of interest and adventure—it will never be dull.

XXXI. HOW TO NAME CHILDREN

AS A CHILD IS NAMED, SO IS HE THROUGH LIFE

It is the higher law that our children should be heirs to the ages' gain; which means they should have the benefit of our wisdom.

All children choose to be born. There is always a covenant between children and parents. The children always come to the parents who will be able to give them the next step in their unfoldment. They bring all of themselves along, and they work out whatever they can in company with their parents who are part of their own Karmic Law.

Often, when they are grown, children say, " If my parents had give me more opportunity," " I never have had the same chance that others have—my parents never understood me." " I had to leave home," " I never had a real mother." " My father was unjust to me." " I never had a fair chance when I was young." These are the complaints of the novitiates—those who do not know.

Every limitation into which we are born belongs to our past thinking and acting. It is a thing that we set for ourselves and it is just what our own soul needs to develop it. Therefore, complaints are useless and deeper understanding is imperative.

The *initiation* and *soul numbers* of the child are the important things to consider in naming it. What sort of character do we want to emphasize? Do we want a 1, 2, 3, 4, 5, 6, 7, 8, or 9? We must study the meanings of the numbers and select a name that will let our child express the strongest soul part of itself.

A woman said, " I want a statesman. I don't want a religious highbrow, nor a dull, plodding scientist. I want a big, strong, physical-mental son—states which may fit him to become the President of the United States of America. When shall I conceive, what month and date, and what shall I name him? "

If we consult the meanings of numbers and ruling passions, we can easily find that he might be conceived in a 7 or an 8 vibration. He should be born to total 6 or 22. We must also take note of the conception vibration. In all ways, this is as important as the birth vibration. The birth vibration is movable and filled with possibilities of change of place and environment. The conception date is fixed, unchangeable and unchanging. There is a spring, summer, autumn, and winter of conception, and all conceptions are in the cosmic rhythm of 1 to 9 or the doubles. The *covenant* between parents and children is the Initiation number (total of day, month and year) and parents have somewhere pledged their willingness to help their children learn their initiations.

We should select a name, then, with soul vibrations that represent the ideals of the initiation vibrations.

If he is born in 2, he should have his individuality, his self-esteem, intensified in his soul number. It would help him to have 4, 6, or 8 as a complementary soul number.

It is always better not to have too many given names, and to have them harmonize in vibrations similar in soul numbers. If the ultimate digits of the name and initiation can be made to be similars and complemen-

WESTERN SYMBOLOGY

taries, the child will have a greater chance for harmony than if they are all under the law of opposites.

EXAMPLE

```
J o h n   R o s w e l l   H o l m e s
6            6    5           6    5
6                11               11
```

IF this child's initiation digit is in 6, he will have a happy life. When there are many numbers in the name of the same vibration as the initiation, it leads to peace and harmony. This name has three vibrations of 6 in his soul.

When a child is backward in school it is often better to make up a name of his numbers that vibrate similarly to his studies and to his year number. Choosing the number that vibrates to the thing which he needs.

Henry would make him popular. *Robert* would help him in music or in choir practice. *Elmer* would make him active and individualized in art, history, and languages. *Ted* would give him a restless spirit. If a child was too plodding and heavy, *Ted* would lighten the weight of his soul. *Emma* would tend towards the domesticity and love of home. *Mary* would help in individualization, order, and independence. *Grace* would tend towards domesticity, adaptability, and charm.

It is the new vibrations of the soul numbers that bring about the change in the child. *Every time we speak a name, we send the vibration through the one who owns it.* It makes a good deal of difference whether we vibrate to Rob or to Jack, to Maude or to Jane. *Physical and mental changes begin with a change of vibrations.* Philip was said to be the name given by mothers to children who were not strong. The two 7's intensified their strength, the two 9's softened their soul life, and the two 3's helped expression. In naming children, parents always unconsciously emphasise the vibrations which seem most worth while to them. It is interesting to note how frequently, when a child is grown and leaves home, he assumes some new combination of vibrations or drops a name altogether.

Many people have more than one given name which they never use. They pour all their vibrations through one name or through one or two initials. J. G. Sylvester is the name in which James Gregory Sylvester has concentrated on individuality and universality. This is his point of greatest power, and he feels it is all he wants to express.

SUMMARY

IN naming children, *first* select the soul-quality you wish to have the children express. *Second,* have few names, and have these in concord with themselves and also in concord with the surname and initiation. Select the soul number in the law of similars or complementaries with the initiation number.

Avoid all combinations of opposites. If the ego has experiences to meet, make him all odd or all concords. He will recombine his name as he becomes an adult, but he will have all the harmony of his youth to safeguard him, and his reason will take care of his experiences as they come to him in adult life.

WESTERN SYMBOLOGY

THE TWO DOORS

XXXII. THE FIRST AND LAST LETTERS OF NAMES

THE *first* letter of a name gives the clue to the positive character of the name. It is written, " The heart of the Master is where we enter." The entrance into our name is an open door to mastery in the manner specified by that letter.

There are many departments in the " House of Life," and we have to ask, " Is our entry through the ONE, or the MANY, or the ALL?" Where we enter is our registration for self-attainment. We may enter as 1, 2, 3, 4, 5, 6, 7, 8, or 9, and this will, to a degree, colour all our actions. (See table of letters and numbers.)

EXAMPLE

Jane Louisa Skinner. Since Jane enters by J (1), and in the personal vibration, we know that if she lives up to herself she will be individualistic in everything. She will have in herself all the qualities of this letter and number.

We find all the numbers carry a very strong impulse of themselves when we enter through them. If we know the meaning of numbers we can easily tell just what we carry with us as the swaddling clothes of our human journey. We are wrapped around with the vibrations of our entrance number and these vibrations never cease while we live. They are really the ray of light with which we light our personal pathway.

The *last* letter of our name tells the vibration in which we shall be when we have lived all the experiences which our name brings to us. Jane ends in E (5). Louise also ends in E (5). *Skinner* ends in R (9). When Jane Louise has worked through to finals she will find herself in freedom and love, because 5 represents personal freedom and 9 symbolizes the " Great Lover."

It is always well to take the entering and closing vibrations into consideration when balancing a name for finals, for they give an unfailing clue to points of character.

XXXIII. THE CIPHER VIBRATIONS

WE find the *Sunday* of life everywhere. There is a respite and a rest for all creation—why not for man? When we know how to read the record of all things we find there is a rest and a reward. If we look for them, we shall find them.

In the numbers 10, 20, 30, and so forth, we have the Sundays of human effort. The cipher is the respite for man in his struggle upward. It means the chance not to hustle: it is void and virgin life. We can make it all or nothing. It is the vibration in which, if we are wise, we will not seek—we will *be*. Our hearts can reap what they have sown, and garner up our fruit of love, joy, and peace. The cipher is the halfway house. Here we can stop, and, in introspection and reflection, we can look over our past, present, and future, and decide what we will keep or discard.

All numbers carrying a cipher are *transition numbers*. The number 1 with a cipher (10) is transmuting to 11; and 2 with a cipher (20) is transmuting to 21. In this silent pause from strife, the ego-man has a chance to select, to rearrange and to discard whatever material is useless in his consciousness or life.

Each cipher *added* means more presents, so if we meet a cipher, we are bound to be on the path of possession. When we know that a cipher means the frictionless way, we can stand still and fear not, and watch for the salvation that our own law will bring to us. We should sit through the vibrations of the cipher like a king with a sceptre in his hand, and live in peace, prosperity, and perfect satisfaction.

The cipher is always the symbol of Divine protection. "There is a rest prepared for the people of God." They enter into rest and cease from their work as He ceased from His. This is the message of the cipher. While in itself it seems nothing, in combination it means the satisfaction of the vibration symbolized by the companion number.

Whenever we see a cipher attached to a number, we know that this is the hour for the fruits of that number. To illustrate: 30 means the perfect personal expression. The soul of the vibration of 3 will be fulfilled to its highest. Or, take 60. Here we find that the love of home, children, domesticity and respectability will be accomplished to the heart's desire—the cup pressed down and running over.

This holds good with all the numbers. Instead of the cipher meaning the *absence of all*, it is the first symbol of the Universe in which *all is*. It is the gift of the Universe to man—the Universal storehouse which can never be exhausted. It comes to us because in the processes of living we have met the law that brings it to us ,and we have won the rest that is prepared for us.

XXXIV. INTENSIFIED NUMBERS

THE numbers 3, 7, and 9 are very important. They represent the closing of the vibrations ahead of them and the inclusion of all that has preceded.

Number 3 is the intensification of 1 and 2, and has latent within its vibrations all that these numbers signify. We find that we come more quickly into the possession of our desires through 3 than we do through either 1 or 2. All our self-expression becomes more complete and satisfactory, and we can be sure that the cycle of 3 will close some personal experience which is more often pleasant than unpleasant. Number 3 is the final grade of the creative, personal, initiative self.

Number 7 is the final of race consciousness, the submerged self and the end of the impersonal path. Number 9 is the final of the ALL and stands at the last *examination*. Wherever these letters are found, either as a digit of personality, soul, destiny, or initiation, their full value must be remembered.

Intensified, number 7 always closes the doors of the outer world for us and crowds us inward. A 7 person holds in his soul all the experiences of the vibrations behind him. It is the closing door of race consciousness—he has again come into himself, plus the experiences of 1, 2, 3, 4, 5, and 6. He is alone, but he must not be lonely or he will miss his grade.

Number 7 has always been the number of the mystics, for at this point of unfoldment the human makes contact with the divine. Every cycle of 7 is a closer contact with the inner self. Numbers 7, 14, 28, 35, 42, 49 and 56 are all steps upon the mystical path to conscious union with the divine. Number 7 tells of wisdom. When the number symbols of the heart of the God-man or REAL SELF is 7, it has been said,

" He is then a well of great wisdom—wear out his doorsill." Number 7 always means the *journey inward*. It comes as a surprise to many when they find that the whole journey of the human life is not outward but inward, and that the only purpose of external action is to gather the experiences whose essence we take inward with us.

Number 9 is the greatest intensified number and in it we have the whole shaft of vibrations. Number 9 contains what no other numbers contain—the whole, and it is capable of refracting into 1, 2, 3, 4, 5, 6, 7 or 8 at any moment. That is why those who have 9 in their hearts are so hard to understand. They are so versatile that they escape from anyone or anything. They belong to *all*, and not to anybody; yet, they can in an instant be wholly manifested in the consciousness of the 1, and as instantly again return to the qualifications of 9.

Number 9 is often called the number of the faithless, because of its versatility and its power to change from the universal to the personal. All the number symbols of the other vibrations will become absorbed in 9. All people of all numbers love them, and it is not always easy to tell just who has the heart of a 9 because this heart is in so many hearts and so many hearts are in it.

Like the dove of the deluge, sometimes a 9 has nowhere to lay his head. However, he is the final of race consciousness and has in himself all that others have, and more; for he has passed through love to God, to man, and to himself, and in his being there throbs the pulse of the unborn race.

Intensified beyond the imagination of the rest of the world, 9 is the open door between earth and heaven. When 9 is reintensified, all is known and expressed, finished, possessing all, creating all, distributing all, in a divine almightiness.

XXXV. PLANETS AND NUMBERS

We find that all numbers and things are in harmony. Each of the nine planets is given a number:

1. Sun
2. Moon
3. Jupiter
4. Uranus
5. Mercury
6. Venus
7. Neptune
8. Saturn
9. Mars

Your planet will be the one bearing the same number as your own soul vibrations. If your soul number is a double number, you must reduce it to a digit, as 11=2—the Moon; 22=4—Uranus. But this enters the field of astrology, and not numerology.

XXXVI. PET NAMES AND THEIR MEANINGS

It is a natural thing to shorten the name of one we love into some more personal vibration. This seems to bring the loved one closer to us and make him (or her) more truly our own. Psychologically, it is true. If we study the soul vibration of the new pet name, we find it expresses in vibration just what the owner of the name means to us.

One man who loves home and children, calls his wife " mate " because she means that to him. The soul vibration of the name " mate " is 6, the number symbol of home and children. Another man calls his wife

"Ve." He wants a pal with whom he can ride, walk, and swim. The soul of "Ve" is 5, the real chum.

A certain man who craved unlimited freedom called his wife "Slim." Later he complained that she was too universal, although every day he vibrated her into the soul of universality. The heart of "Slim" is 9, whose slogan is "All thine, not mine."

Our own pet names reveal to us just where we stand with our friends, and exactly what they expect of us.

For example, the soul number of darling is 10. One with this pet name will naturally want to be the only one in the loved one's life, the director and protector— the one who leads and helps them.

If our pet name is Sweetheart (soul number 16=7), we want to close the loved one in—one world and only two people in it.

Sweetie (24=6) indicates marriage and respectability.

Dearest (11) means that in the loved one we find life, love and God.

Through pet names we touch the souls of those we love and call their love to us, welding it closely by the loving vibrations of our spoken word.

XXXVII. THE RULING PASSIONS OF HUMANITY

The ruling passions are the very deeps of our desires expressed in the numbers of our name.

We may have but *one* number of a kind, or we may have *many* numbers of the same kind. When we have many numbers of the same kind, our likes and dislikes are very intensified; we have some hobby or are more than ordinarily interested in the things which these numbers symbolize. Almost everyone does some *one* thing better and more frequently than he does other things; and likes certain things better than other things. A man's intensified numbers are the signals of his ruling passions. It is the sign that he may follow these things almost to the point of eccentricity.

Sometimes there are no special vibrations in the name. The numbers are equally distributed. This means that the person is about equally developed in his desires, has no ruling passions, and will not run to a tangent in anything. He is not taking any of his initiations over, except as they appear in his ultimate numbers.

There are very many sayings which tell of the ruling passions of people. " You never know what Jim will do . . . he is so eccentric." " There is no use asking John about it . . . he will follow his own opinion." " Oh ! don't expect anything of Henry . . . he has his own hobby." " Mary will never change her plans." " Harriet is bound that she right . . . nothing can convince her otherwise."

THE LOVE STORY OF THE WORLD

The numbers repeated over and over in a person's name indicate his ruling passions. When we know what the numbers mean, we can easily determine how he will conduct himself.

The soul number is final and tells *just* what sort of a person we are, but it does *not* tell what our hobby is. No matter what we are in soul, we must have something that especially interests us, something with which we can keep inspired and busy.

Human consciousness is very complex—more than a simple equation—but when we know our ruling passions, we can turn all our energies toward accomplishment along these lines. When we know our own or another's ruling passions, we are safe from confusion; for we may be sure that we and others will act along the line of least resistance. We need not be disappointed in anyone. People show us in thousands of ways what they are. When we can read the story of the *self*, we can find some point of contact in which we can be harmonious and comfortable.

EXAMPLE

C-L-E-M-E-N-T H-E-D-G-E-S M-O-R-T-I-M-E-R
3 3 5 4 5 5 2 8 5 4 7 5 1 4 6 9 2 9 4 5 9

A fine example of many vibrations! It contains all of the cosmic numbers (1 to 9), and we may expect to find the character very complex. Mortimer would indeed be difficult to understand, if we could not know his ruling passion. However, we see that he has six 5's and four 4's, making 5 the ruling passion. He must be free, or no longer be, although his 4's call him back to responsibilities. But 5, the ruling passion, is uppermost, and we can expect the things of 5 to come forth in Mortimer.

WESTERN SYMBOLOGY

When any number or letter appears more than once in our names, it is a sign that we have taken the initiation over again. Some names have similar number symbols, that is, L and L, R and R, E and E, etc., etc. All double letters mean repetition of the same experiences plus all things of the inner life.

It takes some egos a longer time to pass their grade than others require, but not one jot or tittle of the law will pass away. Only one hundred per cent. of fitness will let us pass on into a new experience.

EXAMPLE

W-I-L-L-I-A-M
5 9 3 3 9 1 4

This name holds the initiations of 9 and 3 taken over twice. It has taken more than one life for William to learn perfected Self-expression and universal love, hence his ruling passion must now be these very things.

We will pass nine times through the nine vibrations unless we extract the qualities of consciousness which they contain in the first round. We will do this in every race—black, red, brown, yellow, and white. That is why eternity must be a long time. We can finish any grade at any time that we step up in our consciousness. By the law of involution we can always hurry and finish in the first round. No one but ourselves can force us to drag, and dragging on through several initiations of the same thing is always a symbol of spiritual slacking. Many numbers of the same kind in our name prove that we have failed to pass in the qualities of consciousness they represent.

XXXVIII. THE RULING PASSIONS OF MEN

(BODY, MIND, SOUL, AND SPIRIT)

1

A MAN with many vibrations of 1 in his composite number is positive and executive. He is dictatorial, sure, often stubborn, and he resents being influenced or directed. He keeps himself separate and does not work well with others. In his own mind he has few equals. Generally he is much nicer to those who are beneath him in rank or intellect than he is to those above him. In business the 1 will often surround himself with a group of " negatives " who are willing to serve him—content to be used and directed by him—and delighted to burn incense at his shrine.

The number 1 man has an individuality that can easily lead him to conceit—he is so very efficient in everything. He is a born leader, director, controller. As long as things please him, he is affable and polite, but he can be hard and almost insolent when he is displeased. When thwarted in his endeavours, he can be tyrannical and revengeful. When aggravated, he can become an agitator. Number 1 is always strong and useful, but he is not often loved just for his own sake. He makes a good friend and will play fair in business and friendship, but he is too self-centered to be a good lover and husband. He generally marries a woman of a submissive temperament. There cannot be two " bosses " in one family. Number 1 *will* be boss. If he marries an independent woman, trouble will ensue until he learns to live the true life.

All places of big achievement belong to number 1. When he is big enough to live on the crest of a power individuality, nothing is too good for him to possess. "All the world falls into line with the man who declares himself a master," and then keeps the laws of a true master-soul.

Number 1 is proud and apt to be very good to those who do not belong to him, but more or less indifferent to his own folk. His children interest him more as they get older. He dislikes little vexations and worries. He is not a natural husband, but his home and family represent one of his ambitions. He is proud to say, "This is my son," or "my daughter" when they are older and represent something worth while.

The 1 is careful in his personality, strong, plain, and original, but attractive. He sometimes approaches loudness, is proud of his own achievements and delights in original ideas, action and display.

SUMMARIZING the 1, we find that in masculinity he means the real self-contained, the *All* in the Self. He is a pioneer who dares to do and to be. He glories in the new and unconventional. He can pull things from obscurity to fame. Always he knows a way out for himself and for others. He is trustworthy in his opinions, and where he leads—it is safe to follow. His ruling passion is *authority*. The world can say:

"*He is a fearless conqueror.*"

2

A MAN with many 2's in his composite name will find his masculinity very different from that of Number 1. Number 2 is very strong in some ways and very weak in others. He can be malleable and yielding, yet diplomatic and " with a false key of seeming weakness take the stronghold of his enemies." Never does he give offence. The ancients said that 2 was the first vibration of a liar, for his very attribute of harmlessness puts him into such a negative condition of character that he will attempt to get peace at any price—he will lie out of his troubles rather than face them.

The 2 makes a delightful friend, agreeable, lasting, non-resistant. Some may think him unreliable because of his non-resistance, but a true 2 *always knows* how, when and where to speak.

The 2 is misunderstood because life has strange values to him. He works out some code which is unfamiliar to the positive brusque minds. He has his own notions of time, hence he can be late with impunity. He never puts the same value on place, position or person that is expected of him.

In personality, the 2 is colourless and never attracts attention. He is careless in clothes and can be very happy in any environment. He is a natural father, fond of home life, and, of all men, he is most miserable when alone.

Often the 2 marries a woman older than himself—one who is positive in his own qualities. However, he can get on with any sort of woman better than any of the other numbers can, for he finds no trouble in matching people's moods. Many times his softness turns away wrath.

The 2 thrives on praise and admiration but is not ambitious. He personifies affection and inspiration, but is unable to do much that is great without help from his friends. However, he has many fields of usefulness. He may be a musician, sculptor, writer, or perhaps a farmer. Landscape gardening appeals to him. Rarely does he accumulate a fortune, for he is more or less of a spendthrift; but he often marries into money or inherits it.

The 2 may fail to make a success of his life by being over sensitive. He may be what is called " touchy " or he may be so " spiritually soft " that he is turned inside out by every word of praise or condemnation.

SUMMARIZING, we would say that the 2 is the " Great Soul " and the soft pedal of the world. He is a pause after strife—a sort of Pool of Siloam where tired minds can come and go away seeing. His ruling passion is *diplomacy*. He keeps others upon the path of self-revelation and they find in him a new hope—a new life and a new faith in humanity. The world can say: " *He laid down his life for his friends.*"

3

THE NUMBER 3 is the symbol of a fine and strong individuality. A man with many 3's in his name is a jolly good fellow, decent, free, happy and ready for anything that life has to offer him. The 3 is a sure cure for the blues. Discouraged people flock to him. Moping is not in his creed.

Three is a scattering number that inclines to general giving and high living. It is hard for a 3 man to accumulate money. He scatters his energy, words and love all over the world. He is loyal to his ideals, but one of his ideals is change and self-expression.

The 3 never asks too much in return for what he does; for since he wants self-expression himself, he is willing to allow it to others. He is not afraid of losing; if he faces arrears, he simply waits and gathers himself together again. The 3 is often down—but never out.

The 3 personality is attractive, charming, even fascinating, which is the cause of some of his greatest weaknesses. He is so popular that he becomes conceited and self-righteous. He is the first degree of the "Great Lover" who is perfected in the 9. Of course, he has some streaks of unfaithfulness in his character which he can strengthen or discard. However, his attentions from all women make it difficult for him to be strong. He attracts all women to him, and he is generous to all.

The love of the 3 finds in home, wife, and family his best form of self-expression. His children are his delight and they love him to distraction. Even while they constitute only one of his forms of self-expression, he never neglects his children. The 3 often marries very young. If he marries one of his own kind, they simply laugh through life. If he marries unhappily, he does not let that bother him—he has too many ways for self-expression to mope because of losing one.

If the 3 will remain true to his type, he cannot miss finding his right occupation, success and fame. The world wants inspiration, and joy and laughter. It pays tribute to the hopeful spirit and encouraging words of the 3. His smile can lighten many a cloudy situation.

SUMMARIZING, the 3 is the "Heart of Life." His greatest accomplishment is to keep happiness alive in the world. Humanity progresses in the ratio of its inspiration. The 3, with the life in his step, the courage in his heart, the song on his lips, and the light in his eyes, is a beacon to those who are on uncharted seas. His ruling passion is inspiration. The world can say:

"*He gave me new life.*"

4

WHEN we find the 4 many times in a name and initiation, we know that the solidarity of the person will command our respect. Four is the foundation of life. A 4 man is the rock of life. He is often forced by some accident to become the support of many, and he is nearly always ready for some unexpected responsibility.

The 4 is always full of self-denial. Self-depreciation is continually in the mouth of a negative 4. He disciplines himself and likes to discipline others. He arises early in the morning to fulfill supposed duties and will resent the fact that others do not follow his example.

The 4 is a non-conformist. He is a lawgiver, and sometimes constitutes himself judge and jury.

The 4 personality is plain and severe, correct and slightly neutral. He is fond of home life. His whole interest centers in the welfare of those who belong to him and he literally slaves for them. His struggle to give everything to those whom he loves often makes him almost a stranger in his own home.

The 4 is industrious and mental, not sentimental. He is faithful to friends and to his employers. He is important in all organizations, but is often too narrow to have the really larger vision. He is a *follower* in the footsteps of those who have gone before and abhors big changes. The slogan, "I sold goods to your grandmother," must have been the brain wave of a 4.

Always proud of his permanency, the 4 makes a faultless and constant husband. He often marries a woman of opposite tendencies who learns after awhile to live her own life and to let her absorbed husband plod on at his own pace.

SUMMARIZING, we find Number 4 is the backbone of

the world; the solidarity of society and business. His eternality is refreshing. Other numbers may come and go, but the 4 will never let us die alone. His ruling passions are *service* and *organization.* The world can say for him:

"*He kept my faith in humanity.*"

5

FIVE is the vibration of life more abundant. The 5 man is useless unless unbound by faction or creed. Freedom is his code; he wants to do *what* he wants, *when* he wants, and *as* he wants,—and he is always trying to do this. The positive 5 knows *how* to do as he pleases without displeasing others.

The 5 is unconventional, although in his soul he is sensitive to criticism. He is always pleasure loving, self-indulgent, and fond of change and travel. He is a great lover of art and is devoted to entertainment and music. He is fond of food, wine, and women. He follows naturally in any avenue which offers him new sensations, more life. If others expect him to be home-loving and responsible, they will be disappointed. He is nearly always athletic. Dancing, swimming, walking, riding, and, in fact, all sports appeal to him.

The 5 is emotional and physical. He is a lover of *many*, but not often a really good husband. His marriages are sudden and sometimes brief. He is not a natural father. He loves a wife, but abhors a mother. Children annoy him and are unnecessary to his happiness.

In personality the 5 is dashing, often pretentious and always obvious. He likes good clothes and wears them well.

His talents are best employed by big firms and institutions; he detests small things. Permanency and waiting are his greatest tests. He is a good investor for quick returns—a natural gambler who will take *one* chance on *anything*. He feels the only thing that pays for living is *freedom,* and he insists on coming and going as he pleases. He may be an investigator, explorer, navigator, adventurer, or " soldier of fortune."

SUMMARIZING, the 5 is a changeless changer. He knows how to let go and still to retain. He wins by forging ahead. His ruling passion is *change*. The world can say:

" *He let the dead past bury its dead.*"

6

A MAN with many vibrations of 6 is the exact polar opposite of a Number 5. He loves home, responsibilities and possessions. He is naturally a marrying man. There is nothing he likes so well as to have a companion, home and friends. His family fills his life —body, mind and soul! He rejoices in his ability to say " ours." He likes respectability, is a traditional " moralist," and is naturally quiet.

The 6 is generous, honest, trustworthy—and always thinking of others. His life is bound up with the Many, so by helping others he helps himself best. The 6 finds it hard to keep " standardized." He can tear down in appearance very quickly, and is apt to become careless with his personality. He is fond of ease and has the courage of his comforts.

The 6 is very gentle and attractive in manner; easily approached—he makes everyone feel at home quickly. Nearly all women like him, and he enjoys their approval.

He knows much of all things, but the 6 is not a revelator—he is an interpreter. He never *creates* big things, but he *gets* big things by his unfailing attention to little things.

The 6 is successful, confident, and sure along his own line of endeavour.

SUMMARIZING, the 6 is the " Great Father," the man that children love, the man with pure ideals! He is the cornerstone of holy matrimony—the man who lives to bring civilization nearer to perfection through the homes of the world. His ruling passion is love of possessions. The world can say:

" *He is the fireside of the race.*"

7

THE VIBRATIONS of a masculine 7 are difficult to understand. He is separate, silent and introspective. His strength is in silence and meditation. He is learning the lesson which many have not learned, the one of holding his tongue. The 7 is the priest number, and a 7 man must keep secrets. He must be still and know that all is good.

The 7 is strong, steady and worth holding on to. When he does talk, he speaks wisely. He is trustworthy and kind, and has a refined personality that tells of the inbreeding of high ideals. He is very careful of his clothes and likes fine cloth with a smooth surface.

The 7 is not a marrying man, although he may marry to escape his lesson of being alone and not lonely. His is the number of celibacy, and of the lesson of living a self-determined life and finding the power within.

The 7 can save the world by his wisdom and is a wise counsellor with whom the nation is safe. Deep insight and finer correspondence are his priceless jewels—if he keeps his soul unclouded with resistance and sullenness.

Women seek him for his wisdom, but they do not

like his silence and his lack of small talk. He takes everything for granted, but women desire to hear things *over* and *over* again, so they pass him by for those who can *flatter* them.

The 7 does not always know that it is not his place to seek but to stand still and to *attract* the things he wants. He is often melancholy, gloomy, and even self-depreciating.

If the 7 fails to keep his place and becomes a babbler in the wild rush of the outside things of life, he loses his poise and sinks into tangles of growth and experiences from which it is hard to get free.

SUMMARIZING, the 7 is poised, calm and dispassionate, with a depth of character that can only be known through close association with him. He is silent and separate, not from a spirit of " holier than thou," but because of the innate shyness of his soul. He is loving, kind and deeply sympathetic, but dumb in words. He gives and never seems to ask to receive because he does not make himself easily understood. He is a firm friend and we can expect him to be the last at the grave. His understanding silence makes him the Great Judge. His ruling passion is love of the inner things. The world can say :

" *He kept the secrets of Humanity.*"

8

EIGHT is the power vibration. A man intensified in this number will boss everybody he can. An 8 man always lives by the brain and brawn of the world. He can set everyone to work, and he can also do things himself, when necessary.

When positive, the 8 is the Great Director, helping others, pushing them on to greater effort. Where he may lead we may follow—for he has almost perfect judgment in all worldly things. He is always trying to lift himself and others into higher positions of authority and power. When he is negative, he is little more than a big bully, the profiteer who sees the world as full of weak people, fit only to be sweated for his own personal gain. He has yet to learn the law " As ye did it unto the least of these ye did it unto me."

The 8 always commands attention with his *power* personality. He has the fine severity of a 4 stepped up to distinction. He is careful of his appearance, always well groomed and selects clothes suggesting durability.

The 8 loves big things and shuns the tragedy of little things. His zeal and ardour attract all people, and his success inspires others to try again.

The 8 is a good father, and helps those who bear his name to lift it up to some place of authority and power.

SUMMARIZING, the 8 is a true constructionist. The world owes him a great debt for his ever enlarging vision of form, order, and perfected expression. His ruling passion is *to create*. The world can say:

" *He taught me the value of bigness.*"

9

NINE is *The Great Lover*. He is kind, patient, affectionate, and understanding.

He is a true actor, tragedian and comedian,—all in one. When he laughs the world laughs *with* him. He is genial and forgiving—he is the very heart of attraction.

The 9 is a marrying man; he loves all kinds of women —the whole sex is his creed of love and admiration.

Nine in masculinity needs a fixed point of attraction to bring out the best that is in him. He demands a legitimate outlet for his affections or he grows too detached and careless. Nine is called the vibration of faithlessness on the negative side, because it makes for too much inclusion—it is not the *One* but the *Many*.

The 9 man is open to many influences; and, as he is soft, fine and sympathetic, he is apt to be too easily influenced unless he is in the positive 9 vibration.

The 9 has a charming personality which is softened by curves. He is not too fastidious, but he selects clothes with soft, smooth surfaces and of flexible quality in which he looks comfortable and easy.

SUMMARIZING, the 9 is the Great Lover of the world. He is close enough to God not to be mistaken; and he is close enough to men not to be misunderstood. His ruling passion is *love of humanity*. The world can say:

"*He has an understanding heart.*"

11

THERE are only two of the double vibrations important enough to demand special interpretation. These are 11 and 22. All the others (33, 44, 55, 66, 77, 88 and 99) can be interpreted as vibrations which are merely intensified in their own substance.

Number 11 is a spiritual grade in individuality. It is the personal 1 added to the universal 1. The man with many vibrations of 11 will be interested in mysticism, but he will not be as powerful in controlling the things of the outer world.

The 11 is a dreamer, a seeker after causes. He is a poet and a priest of the Inner Temple, the guardian of the Holy of Holies. When negative, the 11 is like an unfrocked priest, and of all men he is then the most miserable in conscience. Because of his great perception and cunning, he knows the finer forces and can use them for his own benefit, and he may sacrifice others to his own ends.

When positive, the 11 is the great transcendentalist, the mystic in the shrine of Life. He keeps God alive in the minds of the world. He is the minister, the religious educator, the supreme idealist, the man with a vision.

In personality the 11 is much like the 1. He is distinguished but not handsome.

The 11 is not a marrying man; <u>children tire him</u>. He knows how to be alone and not lonely, for he is, in himself, the dual ONE. Marriage for 11 is always risky. He can live with almost anyone; but few can live with him in perfect comfort, because he is so standardized in his own high ideals that he finds it hard to surrender to the uninitiated.

SUMMARIZING, the 11 is the messenger, and his message is of God and about the good. He keeps the human mind turned towards Heaven. He stands for love, mother, home, and future; and he carries in his consciousness the light that never dies, the light which lighteth every man who cometh into the world. His ruling passion is *uplifting humanity*. The world can say:

"*He helped me meet life fearlessly.*"

22

TWENTY-TWO is the double vibration of association, sensitiveness, and diplomacy. With all its vibrations added, it is 4. Therefore, we find in it the plus material substances, which makes it a tower of strength and understanding.

The 22 is the master builder, the great constructionist,

and he helps all the other numbers to lift themselves into finer form and better privileges.

The 22 is something like Number 8, but when he is negative he has a longer arm and a stronger will to work iniquity. Few, except those of his own kind, have enough strength of character to stand up against him. He will rule; or, if opposed and the least bit negative, he will ruin.

The 22 is splendid in personality. He is a power man, a power thinker, a power salesman, a power builder. He always attracts by his personality and makes good through his efficiency. He is not always careful in the selection of his clothing, but he always looks well dressed and at ease. He is naturally fond of heavy textures and semi-rough surfaces.

The 22 is a marrying man. When he is not rightly mated he will be a boss, not a lover. He is fond of children; for, as with number 8, his children feed his ambition. He takes good care of everybody and everything that belongs to him because it adds to his popularity.

The 22 is ambitious, eager and urging. Life must give him great things or he is never satisfied. He is always a leader. He avoids working for others. When he does work for others, he quickly reaches the top places. He can see through a material situation quickly, but is slow on transcendental wisdom. His five senses are his best guide and he trusts them.

Twenty-two has the world in the hollow of his hand if he knows his own powers and uses them constructively.

SUMMARIZING, the 22 is the supreme materialist, the

power-man of the number vibrations. He knows his work and can do it. He works from the love of creating rather than from the love of people or things. His ruling passion is *ambition for the highest*. The world can say of him:

"*He taught mankind to dare and to do.*"

XXXIX. THE RULING PASSIONS OF WOMEN

(BODY, MIND, SOUL, AND SPIRIT)

1

A WOMAN whose vibrations are in the majority of 1 will be very hard to understand. She has so much in her that is unexpressed. If she is positive she is often brusque, dominant, and sometimes borders on arrogance. If she is negative she is self-sympathetic and never penitent. She is kind and loving by spells, and again she is almost cold, silent and separate.

The 1 is *mentally* loving and spiritual. She detests display of emotion, and strives not to forget her dignity. She is ambitious, and likes authority, recognition and appreciation.

The 1 is sometimes the best sort of a pal, chummy and strong. She doesn't ask for anything she cannot give. She is honourable and always does her share. She will pay her debts and is independent and self-contained.

The 1, when she is too dominant and personal, is often an inexorable boss. She is not a naturally domesticated woman, but can manage a home very well. It is not the height of her ambition to be too domestic. She marries her opposite and, sometimes, if she is very positive, her husband is what other men call "henpecked."

Physically she is attractive, although more from her air of strength than because of her real beauty. She is athletic and loves outdoor things. She wears her clothes well, and dotes on distinctive things. She is not attractive to women but is liked by men. Her mental charm is as intense as is the physical charm of other numbers.

The 1 is too practical to be romantic; and, emotionally, too inert to be deeply religious. She is queen in her own domain of intellectuality. She is super-sophisticated. The weak fear her.

The 1 always dislikes patronage. Although almost everyone respects her, but few really love her. She is more often the master than the mate. She is born to lead and to command. Few can stand the searching criticism of her mind, for there are few who want to be eternally criticized. Her inborn superiority is more likely to exile her than to make her popular. She hews to the line in speech and in action and lets " the chips fall where they may."

SUMMARIZING, the 1 is a strong, independent, steadfast woman. When she lives up to herself she is a splendid pioneer woman whose zeal and courage have made many things possible for others too weak to do them for themselves. There is no turning back to the 1; it is always the knife to the hilt. The erring must look well to themselves, for they will certainly meet her scorn, and oft-times her pity—but not her pardon. True to her instincts, the path of the 1, is just as that of the sailor who tracks the polar star. Her ruling passion is *power*. The world can say of her,

" Her courage is majestic."

WESTERN SYMBOLOGY

2

THE WOMAN who has for her dominant vibrations the number symbol of 2 is the sort of person we never remember, and to whom we must be introduced every time we meet. She has no distinctive qualities which attract our attention. If we noticed her at all it is rather for the absence of interests than for their presence.

The 2 is nearly always colourless—unimportant—even if she, in the positive side of her vibrations, is gentle, kind, unobtrusive, non-resistant and lovable. If negative, she is simply non-existent and receives little response from life.

The 2 is very often overlooked—pushed back by every other dominant number. They are made to eat the crumbs that fall from full tables. Unless they really assert themselves they will remain unknown until some other person pushes them to the front.

The 2 always attracts friends. It is through her friends that her genius becomes known, and she reaps the reward of her own merit.

The 2 is very neutral in her personality—often pretty in a self-effacing way. She cannot be made to show off. Many dollars may be spent on her and she will be no better than before. She looks just as well in the commonest clothes as in the finest. Clothes make some men and women, but they do not help the 2 to be anything save the 2.

The 2 detests rising to big, stirring, public things. Obscurity is her keynote. She prefers to be the force behind; never the force in front. She is kind, sweet, gentle, loving, devoted to her friends and children—a natural mother—generous of time, love, money and strength.

The 2 attracts all kinds of people, and is a harmonizing influence in any crowd. " Blessed are the peacemakers, for they shall inherit the earth " must have been meant for these. The people of the 2 vibration follow, but never lead—except in the things of their own world. Theirs is the last word; never the first. It may be said of the 2 that her children rise up and call her blessed. Her submissiveness is her chief attraction.

The 2 often attracts dominant men because of this very quality. They are the type of whom men say, " she rests me." She asks nothing and gives all.

SUMMARIZING the 2, one can say 2 is always a " house of refuge." She is the first at the cradle and the last at the grave. She is faithful and loving unto the end, asking no reward, but taking the love of doing as the best reward. Unsung, often unpraised—all battles are fought for her, never by her. Her ruling passion is *adaptability*. The world can say,

" She taught me the spirit of gentleness."

3

THE vibrations of a woman whose majority numbers are 3 is a very easy one. She loves life, pleasure, laughter and easy things. She is the butterfly of the world, and never takes on too much responsibility. To her nothing really matters—or, at least, not for long.

When 3 is positive and normal she loves to sip the honey from the flowers of life, and her only guide is her personal desires. She loves the beautiful and artistic almost to a fault, and if she has a weakness it is on the side of her indulgence in the vibrations of beauty and harmony.

The 3 cannot show forth her best in an unlovely environment. Unless she is happy she will pine and mope away her time and energy. She loses her genius under repression. She will put forth all her effort to accomplish the thing that pleases her, but she will fall flat before some dull expression.

The 3 is always beautiful physically if she lives up to her law. Hers is the beauty of personality, and nothing can spoil her charm. The 3 has grace of form, charm of manner and she possesses the most physical beauty of all numbers. The 6 comes second and 9 is third.

The 3 has a great ego, but when negative she is filled with personal pride. She will always justify herself in every way, and sometimes even when she is in the wrong, she can force the other one to apologise to her.

The 3 at once forgives herself for any transgression and cannot hold a grudge against anyone for long.

The 3 is an artist, an entertainer. The whole world of entertainment and amusement is open to her. She is a fine and jolly friend—never dull.

The 3 can wear almost any style of clothes and get by with it better than any other number. She is always careful with her person, and can be vain and a bit showy. She is a natural coquette. She loves admiration, romance, and is sentimental and fond of fashion. She loves jewellery and adornment.

The 3 attracts all kinds of men, for she is a jolly companion. She is a good mother, and regards playing with her children as the best method of bringing them up. She is often profligate in her generosity—scattering by nature. She finds it hard to accumulate.

The 3 is welcome anywhere. She is never tiresome, always tactful. Charming and genial; she wins the world by her smile and camaraderie.

SUMMARIZING the 3, we know that she is joy, laughter and lightheartedness, and she stands supreme. The 3 lives naturally in a joy-world, welcome with people in situations that are always all right. It takes great opposition and repression to check the bubbling spring of winsome gladness in her soul. Her ruling passion is *happiness*. She is the daughter of glee—the child of sunshine. The world can say,

" Her happiness dried my tears."

4

THE vibrations of a woman of 4 is another story. The 4 is strong, brusque, plain-spoken, and without any frills or deception. She is given to self-denial rather than self-indulgence. She is unromantic, except in a mental way. Sometimes she seems to be too hard and is often unrelenting.

The 4 will adhere strictly to the letter. She rarely departs from the normal. She is always more inclined to do what she ought to do and to live by what she needs, rather than by what she wants. She has very few weaknesses, and often has but little sympathy for those who have.

The 4 is sympathetic in regard to real need, but she is cold against pretension and stupidity. She is honest, industrious, and usually dull. She loves responsibility, and feels slighted if no one asks anything of her.

The 4 wants value received for all she does. She gives generously but expects fair measure in return. Trustworthy and dependable, nevertheless she is sometimes gloomy; always willing to do anything when she thinks it is right but is unrelenting when her suspicions are aroused.

The 4 is physically unattractive. She has something of the distinguished look of the 1, but she is often called "The Plain Jane." She has angles and errors of physical form.

The 4 seldom really plays. Her work and avocation sometimes enslave her. Her self-made responsibilities often break her. She can neglect her personality in the pursuit of duty, which is her supreme ideal. She is not a natural home-maker, for she belongs to the professional or business world.

The 4 has little attraction for men. She is much like the 1—clever and super-sophisticated. She is absorbed in *things* rather than people. In personality she is severe. She selects plain clothes and wears very few frills. No greater contrast can be imagined than that between the personality of 3 and 4.

The 4 is a great organizer and director, a fine clubwoman, and is popular because of her ability. She is the hope of the shirk, and is always overloaded with other people's duties. She lives and dies in perpetual order. Correctness is her code, and she is a pillar of strength wherever she is found.

The 4 wins some of the greatest things of life through her steadfastness to duties that must be done and to ideals which must be sustained.

SUMMARIZING the soul of the 4, we would say that " She is as strong and immovable as Gibraltar, her iron soul never knows defeat, and when the weak of earth need support they find her a Rock of Ages. Staunch and unchanging as some tall pine that braves the elements and lifts through all the storm its head sublime, so the 4 keeps true to what she *knows* to be true." Her ruling passion is *Service*. The world can say of her, " She taught me faith in eternalities."

5

THE vibrations of 5 are effervescent and changeful. Her soul loves luxury and admiration. Things can quickly get too slow for the 5. She must be free and any bondage chafes her. She loves her own moods and changes, and will resist all efforts towards permanency. Anything too fixed and certain tires her.

In personality the 5 is always " ultra," no matter what vibration she may have in her soul. If she is 5 she will never be a common type. She can wear her clothes with a grace unknown by the other vibrations. She can look chic in the oldest things.

The 5 loves to depart from the normal or the accepted standard. She is unconventional, and detests a chaperon. The first freedom from the chaperon may probably be laid at her door. She paved the way to a finer individuality.

The 5 loves to break laws—not because they *are* laws but rather because her spirit of liberty resists direction and control. Her spirit of personal liberty is always defiant.

The 5 understands all men and attracts them all. Understanding them is her vocation. Some women know art, others know home, still others know service, but 5 know *men,* and can work her way with them, not so much by efficiency as by persuasion.

The 5 is a good companion. Asking little, giving little, detesting responsibility herself, she hesitates to burden others. She is a marrying woman, but 5 is not the vibration of stable marriages. She is not a natural mother, and children are not necessary to her happiness. The 5 often has more than one husband and sometimes many lovers. She is a good business woman, and is often found in the professions.

Her fine spirit of fellowship makes her an attractive person, and her love of change keeps her from becoming dull and dogmatic. The 5 helps the world to break up all its old fixed points of convention when they should be broken. The 5 " travels light "—body, mind, soul and spirit. She will not drag an old past with her.

The 5 can discard a gown, a home or a friend quickly and make a new contact for her own benefit. She is a good gambler, and will take all sorts of chances on anything that interests her. She is a good pal. She has great understanding, and her ability to play the game of life with no regrets makes her fascinating. " In that give-and-take of glances, kisses sweet as honey dew, when we played with equal chances, did you win or did you lose?" This is the spirit of 5 and to her freedom makes all life more liveable and interesting.

SUMMARIZING 5 we can say she is simply life—and life most abundant. She takes away the dread of the old yesterday and the fear of to-morrow. Life is real and fit to be lived when she lives it *her* way.

Her ruling passion is *perfected personal freedom*. The world can say,

" She taught me new life—the joy of being myself."

6

THE vibrations of a woman whose dominant number is 6 are those which make for home, motherhood and family interests, and her whole soul and mind are centred in these things.

THE LOVE STORY OF THE WORLD

The 6 loves her own vine and fig tree, and the protection which these give. She dreads the larger things of life and turns naturally to those paths in which there is little risk and much protection.

The 6 has very little ambition to conquer anything more than the hearts in her home. She is retiring, full of ideality. She likes to live in the illusions of life, and often thinks life really different from what it is. The 6 always shirks hard and distasteful realities. She likes the *idea* of things better than the things themselves. She is a natural finisher of things, but never a beginner, except of the things which have under them the unfailing foundation of certainty. She is afraid to take a chance.

The 6 is often a "Martha," anxious and troubled about many things. She wants things to be so right that she tires others with her attention. In any situation she would rather be helpful than great.

The 6 has a very pleasing personality when she is positive in her ruling vibration. She has the softened curves of 3, with some of the originality of face and form which is found in 1 and 7. She is motherly in her atmosphere, and she knows the subtle charm of a true motherly face and form.

The 6 attracts all men through her intensified femininity, and her dependence upon them fires their masculinity into a protecting flame. She is clinging, subservient, understanding, faithful, full of service—the very cornerstone of Mother, Home and Heaven—and is "Still loyal though the ruffian smite. Is this weakness? Is it not the love that glorifies?"

All the light of sacred story gathers around the Divine Motherhood of 6. The Jewish proverbs say "God could not be everywhere, so He made mothers."

Out from the soul and the body of a woman there passes the ever extending life of the world. The 6 is the great Mother Conception. All virtues and all vices are her birthright. The whole of creation is in her womb. No voice in all the world is ever raised against the true mother.

SUMMARIZING a 6, we can say that in 6 we find the cosmic cradle, and on her mother heart the whole world rests. Her children in every quarter of the globe rise up and call her blessed. Her ruling passion is *to comfort mankind*. The world can say,

" She is a divine mother."

7

THE vibrations of a 7 woman are those of silence and separateness. She is the well of deep water. No one—not even her own children or her husband—really knows her. She has heard words in the silence that will never bloom into speech. She is in the world, but not of it. She seems to be forever looking on—a visitor—and if anyone expects her to act like some of the other numbers he will be bitterly disappointed, for 7 will always be a 7, and change is no part of her creed.

The 7 is often misunderstood because she cannot express herself. She is sometimes called cold, or proud, or even indifferent, because she does not take part in life as the ordinary world might expect.

The 7 is a calm, dispassionate, independent woman, with some of the qualities of 1. Supremely individualized, if she is true to type—she is easy, restful, and soft of voice and touch.

The 7 has a refined and pleasing personality which does not attract, largely because of her seeming lack of geniality. She is very self-contained and never able to gush or to make-believe. She lacks the gift of small talk unless she is negative. Then she becomes that great failure, a babbling 7, and will lose all her gifts.

The 7 is none too popular with men. They seldom seek her of their own accord. They must first meet her and discover all her deep, loving qualities; then she has the power to keep love and friendship forever. But 7 is not a true marrying number. It is written that this number is the path of the priestesses of the Temple.

The 7 is naturally the true confessional. The ancients hold that 7 was the only woman who could faithfully keep a secret. She is able to hide her own feelings and her own true selfhood from the world. She can also hold everything that comes into her life.

The 7 is the Sphinx of Womanhood, and all of her consciousness is hidden away. Not everyone who runs can read. She is constant, unchanging in her loves and friendships. She is just and of sound judgment, and as unyielding as 1 and as uncompromising as 4, but she is never forgetful nor inconstant.

The 7 has a refined and correct personality and always selects the finest things in clothes, but is never showy. She is as clean cut in looks as in character. Keen of tongue and intellect, she knows *what* she wants and what she *doesn't* want and is artistic in her clothes.

The 7 is the woman who often lives and dies alone. This is not because she is unloved, but because she is a poor mixer and a natural hermit. She detests noise and confusion and loves silence, softness and solitude. The 7 is the true vibration of celibacy. It is not hard for a positive 7 to live alone and not be lonely. The confidences of association often tire her. She is methodical in her habits and does not like interference. The

7 is not a natural mother. To her, children are more of an inheritance than a possession.

SUMMARIZING 7 we find that while the 7 signifies wisdom and aloneness, she is a temple of peace in the babble of tongues. She is rest personified. She is like a cool drink after a hot climb. Her divine repose is a benediction to the weary.

Her ruling passion is *self-realization*. The world can say,

" She always understands."

8

THE woman who is made out of as many vibrations as 8 is strong and positive in her doing. Cheerful, certain, she is the embodiment of courage and can radiate courage to others.

The 8 is often dominant, exacting and egotistical. She KNOWS the things which others only guess. She speaks with authority and not as a weakling. Her strong words help others. " Deep toned, 'pure and true as steel, she rings the chords that bind and heal."

The 8 bosses everybody. She always leads, never follows. She gets quickly to the head of the house of business. Executive, cool-headed and well balanced, she takes all responsibility, and often she is heartily disliked by others for her efficiency.

The 8 can make a situation. And, if let alone, she will make one for others. She loves name, place, power, money and display. Men like an 8 for a companion and a business associate. They admire her as a pal. But men who are strong like herself will never marry her, because there can only be one general in a family of two or in a business. She attracts the gentler types of men, particularly 2, 6 and 11. These seldom please her because they are not successful along the lines of masculinity which she admires.

The 8 can give herself more than a negative or subjective man can give her; and love without money is *not* her code. She has none of the qualities of consciousness which would make love in a cottage attractive to her. This must be left to the 2.

The 8 is a natural mother. She builds bodies with the same grace that she builds other physical things. She is often the mother of statesmen whose brilliancy and greatness is their mother's legacy.

The 8 is one of the strong cornerstones of society, business, and often of the church, for she is a law giver, not a law breaker. She is kind and just to a great extent, but she seldom errs on the side of mercy.

SUMMARIZING 8, she is strength and power plus, and she has attained this through slow self-conquest and comradeship with the things that develop them. No one needs to prate about her weaknesses; they only strengthen her strength. Her ruling passion is *sympathetic self-association for herself and others*. The world can say,

"She is the open door to great opportunities."

9

THE vibration of 9 will give us a woman of a highly intensified type. She is the great philanthropist, the social worker, the leader of welfare clubs, and the director of many humanitarian affairs.

The 9 loves humanity. She is more interested in *people* than in things. She is kind, loving, patient and forgiving, and will often err on the side of mercy. When positive in her number she becomes the missionary, the nun, giving her life for the good of the world.

The 9 has a splendid, attractive personality. She has taken on the appeal of 6 and the curves of 3. Her selection of clothes, home and environment in general is always strong, beautiful and artistic.

All men turn naturally to 9, attracted by her geniality, her love and her sweetness. The 9 is not a marrying number, but she does marry, and often marries very young. The 9 is absorbed in everything. One thing seldom includes enough to satisfy.

The 9 is not happy in just one home, one situation or one sort of place or thing. She is capable of including many things in her life. We find her a member of many clubs, active in outside things of different kinds, all done in the name of humanity, and for its good.

The 9 is dramatic, artistic and musical, and a career or business can easily take the place of a home and children. She is a great tragedienne and sometimes a great comedienne. Her beauty is often so perfect that the world would miss its fairest flower, if left to bloom unseen behind the doors of home.

The world learns greatness from the great, virtue from the virtuous, freedom from the free, and beauty from the beautiful, and a 9 woman, when she is true to her type, has the moulding of the race-mind in her hands. They give all they have to those who have not, and their life is nearly always spent in this urge toward doing and helping. The highest worship of God is service to men, and to be happy the 9 keeps herself in continuous service.

SUMMARIZING 9, we can say that the whole story it has to tell the world is *love*. Love to God, love to men, and to self. And this love is bound up with divine compassion. It is love that lifts mankind up to higher levels of endeavour; and, knowing this, the 9 goes on her way. " Truth, love and peace! This is the soul's true quest, through sun and shadow without bitterness." This is her aim. The world can say,

" Her love redeemed me."

11

The eleven is the vibration of purely religious womanhood. She is not so humanly attached, but is a great idealist and a true worshipper. Her conversation is mostly of God and godly things. She is in the world, but not very much of it.

The 11 is strong and self-reliant like the 1, but filled with the revelation of the last 1. The first Adam was of the earth earthy, the last Adam is a living soul, and 11 is the first and last Adam. She can be an angel or a devil. The 11 is rarely popular in organization. She is too dominant, inflexible, and knows too little of conciliation or surrender.

The ideals of 11 are high. She holds her own life and the lives of others grimly up to impossible standards. She is poetic and artistic, filled with high revelation.

The 11 helps people more by her ideality than by her personality. She is like the 1, distinguished, severe and correct in looks. She attracts men of all ranks by her intellect and spirituality, but they seldom love her bcause men *never* love their masters. They reverence and admire them, but men only love their loves and their mates. And their mates are the women who do not over-reach them physically, mentally, emotionally or spiritually.

The 11 is separated from all men but those of her own vibration. When 11 meets 11 they seldom marry because they have been married before to their ideals;

and they won't leave the impersonal for the personal. The 11 is the last vibration of celibacy, and can be very happy alone.

The 11 has more patience with others than she has with herself. She appears neglected and lonely when she really is not. The 11 is not a natural mother; and she prefers to be the bride of the Lamb rather than of man.

The 11 can be despotic, severe, and often tyrannical. She is so wedded to her ideals that she brooks no interference with any of her plans.

SUMMARIZING the 11, we find that 11 is the " Light of Life," the link between the race and its consciousness of God. " He that followeth me, shall not walk in darkness; He shall have the Light of Life; " and, following the light of the ideal of 11, we grow out of human into divine humanity. Her ruling passion is to *turn men's minds to the great Ideal,* and to *save humanity.* The world can say,

" She taught me how to find God."

22

THIS double vibration of womanhood is like the 8, only plus. It has all that 8 has, and more. The 22 has the whole world in her lap, for she is the master life. She can build and express at will. She is the mind of the home as well as the home itself.

The 22 is sound, fixed, capable. She brooks no contradiction. No one is above her in her own field, no one is beneath her, and no one is beside her except those of her own kind—and these are not competitors.

The 22 seldom needs a counsellor. She is a counsellor. She is back to her source, and her wisdom directs her. She has kept the softness of the 2, the iron hand of 4, the efficiency of 8 and added to it the adaptability of another 2.

The 22 is the head and heart of her environment. She thinks, acts, and chooses. If she is true to her type the whole world leaps to her will.

The 22 has an attractive personality. She is nondescript except in the atmosphere of power and strength; there she is pleasing and radiates efficiency. Men are attracted to her just as they are to the 8, but the same things stand in her way. Men come and go, respect her genius but only awaken her contempt, for *her* code is that love and power must come to her in *one* hand.

The 22 is a ruler, a boss, and will claim recognition. Money is not really her god; but she makes it her necessity. As she wants big material freedom, she makes money the basis of her visions. She is a marrying woman and a natural mother at heart. Married even to an inferior man, her children are often far above the average in physique and intelligence. When properly mated she is the mother of statesmen and leaders.

The 22 is so strong and self-reliant that she seldom asks or seeks sympathy; and, without watchfulness, she can be too hard. The world of opportunity and endeavour is open to her everywhere. Her skilled labour has no competition.

SUMMARIZING, we find that the 22 is simply the foundation stone on which she and others can build sublime things that will stand the test of time. Humanity in its weakness turns to her and finds help. The calm, strong life of 22 calls to humanity to come up higher, to the heights of human consciousness where they will find peace. Her ruling passion is *self-determination*. The world can say,

" In her life I found new life."

XL. PERSONALITY

WHAT WE LOOK LIKE

Life always repeats itself. The tides sweep in and sweep out. Spring passes into summer, summer into autumn, autumn into winter, winter into summer—repeating again and again. In similar manner, the universal intelligence in atom or man goes on repeating.

We began when life began. We are not merely a part of this great universal life. We *are* this life. We are embodied not as atoms alone but as atom, molecule and mass. And this mass is localized intelligence in the cosmic intelligence.

We are deathless souls on an endless journey. Life is always from beginning to beginning again. We have our springtime and our summer, our autumn, our winter—and there is nothing in the universal life that is not in our own.

We began when life began; and we have gone on as life itself, carrying from cycle to cycle all the positive cells of the kingdoms from which we have evolved.

This localized intelligence called "Us" has come through the mineral, the vegetable, the animal kingdoms, up to the kingdom called "Human," and man is on an endless journey toward the levels of embodiment almost unguessed—and certainly unknown.

After man, what? Angels—masters of the spheres—gods of the planets, and on and on. " The path leads up to the eldest Sun where the White Ones go in their holy mating, and the holy Will is done."

We come *from* great worlds of intelligence behind

us, and we go *on* to great worlds of intelligence *ahead* of us. We are a little world in a big world, evolving by natural laws from the vibrations of the *One* to the *Many,* and then to the ALL.

The ego-man is the entity that endures—a permanency in impermanent forms. The kingdoms of consciousness remain the same, but the ego-man goes on, taking with him the derivatives from every plane. A monkey does not become a man, a reptile a fish, or a flower a mouse; but *that life* which embodies in form becomes 1-2-3-4-5-6-7-8-9 in every kingdom of cosmic intelligence from atom to celestial hosts.

Our localized ego-consciousness plunges into form from kingdom to kingdom, and when we reach the kingdom of humanity we arrive with all the consciousness of the path over which we have come. It is latent, not expressed; but it is there to be called upon whenever necessity demands.

Thus we find that our past is as great as our future. And, awakening to consciousness in this life, we can read our past and our future by the number-symbols of our name and birth. It does not happen that one is named John and another George. It does not happen that our final equation shows " 1 " or " 9 " or " 6." These are the measure of ourselves, and, to those who can read the story of our life and actions, they tell an almost forgotten past, and become the blue-print for the future.

We can read our history in the stars. We can read it in our palms. We can read it in the shape of our head, the colour of our eyes and our hair. We can read it in the sound of our voice, and in the number-symbols that make our name. Our personality is our presentation card.

When related to us, every number carries its own registration in form, and it always remains true to its own type. In a basket of apples we may find good, better and best apples—but we never mistake a peach for an apple, for in all its reconstruction an apple could not become a peach. Just so we find that all the numbers 1-2-3-4-5-6-7-8-9 remain the same in character, but they manifest as *positive* and *negative* in form. The 1 will always be 1. Nothing can make it become 2, but it may be a positive or a negative 1, and upon this depends its power and its progress.

Our personality is of supreme importance, as it is our presentation card to life. We should know our type and lift our personality up to one hundred per cent. Care and understanding of our personality is the first step on the path to power.

We must remember that our personality is found by the digit of the consonants in our names—remembering also that this number-symbol shows just what has been back of us. Our *personality* clearly reveals the secret of just how we have lived in the past states of being. If our personality expresses all the harmony and beauty of the number-symbol we may know that we have lived constructively, because we are beautiful. If our personality is inharmonious and has errors of physical angles we may know that our past has been full of tragedy which was so intense that we have passed it into form.

WHAT 1 LOOKS LIKE

EVERY positive 1 has a striking and original personality. They always look *different* from other people. They are dignified; although not so pretty, they are distinguished looking. They are more or less above medium height, and inclined to be thin rather than to be rotund. Sometimes they are even bony.

They are often so pronounced in some original point of face or form that they are really fascinating. They are strong looking, and should attract all weaker persons just from their radiation of strength and power. They have irregularity of physical angles, but these are typical and pleasing.

In dress they are original—sometimes a bit showy—and they love bright patterns. They are as original in their minds as they are in their clothes. A departure from the conventional track may be expected from them.

The negative 1 is marked by the absence of all the positive qualities of 1. They are not at all what they should be. They have no originality. They are not strong characters. They never express themselves, and they look insignificant and aimless when they ought to look strong and attractive. People pass them by because there is nothing of character in their make-up. They are no less mongrel in their clothes than in their characters.

When we say, " He looks like a positive 1," we know we have seen some one with the personality of power, distinction, and originality. Wherever he is or what he does, he never looks common.

When we say " He looks like a *negative* 1," we can find the clue to the limitations he sets for himself. There is no chance for us to fail in our interpretations. Life hangs its signals everywhere. All negative personalities can be changed by just cultivating the positive side of life, and living close to the positive states of mind. We can take on a new personality which will have in it all that it was ever meant to express.

WHAT 2 LOOKS LIKE

THE 2 is in a different class altogether. They are between the 1 and the 3, and this places them in a peculiar position. They are learning the first lesson of "sinking" their individuality. They have not yet come to perfect self-expression. They are submerged with greatness all around them. They cultivate an appearance of submission, and even a positive 2 never looks like a leader.

They are always of a subdued tone and coloring. They look kind, agreeable and non-resistant. They are fond of neutral shades; they are often colorless in their clothes. They are never ultra-fashionable, or very marked in curves or angles. Usually they are a happy medium. They are often heavily set, or plump—not bony.

The positive 2 looks comfortable and easy. They appeal by their restful atmosphere. People are usually fond of them because they do not provoke argument. They never disturb another's fixed ideas. If one would describe them in a few words one would say, "They are soft, appealing and agreeable in their personality."

A negative 2 is a mixture of all of these things with no real point of attraction. They are mixers by nature. They wear clothes of many colours, and can wear old clothes with comfort. That they do not match, or are out of fashion, doesn't matter to a negative 2. They look toneless and slouchy, and they have nothing to recommend them to our attention. They are the people to whom we must be introduced every time we meet. They have little personality or attraction. It was from attempting to describe a negative 2 that the word "frump" was coined. Even with much money and every opportunity, a negative 2 cannot make their personality attractive or beautiful. They tear down easily, and nothing can ever step them up in looks to the satisfactory point which a 3 can maintain without effort.

It is hard for a 2 to look really smart. They cannot show off. Even with expensive outfits they will be quickly effaced by a flashing 5 who is a good bluffer. They have a quiet, kind, nondescript personality which gives a silent message. The world loves them because they have the gentle heart of a saint.

WHAT 3 LOOKS LIKE

THE positive 3 may be poor and have little to make them happy, but it does not affect their looks. Working or resting, playing or not playing, young or old, the personality of a positive 3 is a most valuable asset. Beauty has a great influence upon the minds of the world. Beauty can get in where plainness must remain outside. Beauty gets forgiveness and mercy where ugliness gains justice only. Thus, the 3 triumphs on the physical plane. With the perfect harmony of face and form, the pleasing combinations of colour, the grace of action, the charming curves, the symmetry of motion —the *positive* 3 has the world in its hands; and its personality is its most valuable asset.

Negative 3 is easily identified. Neglect and inharmonious mental states tear down the flesh, line the face, and bend the form. Often one who has 3 in his personality symbol is very unlike the thing he ought to be, but it is only a picture of how far he has departed from his birthright of beauty.

A marked beauty always shines out in a 3, and it takes more than a few slovenly, neglectful years to mar the personality which is built in this vibration.

WESTERN SYMBOLOGY

WHAT 4 LOOKS LIKE

THIS is the plain side of the picture. A *positive* 4 is the one who has given rise to the name " Plain Jane." The 4 is all angles and is apt to be severe in lines. Looking at 4 we would say they are practical in every angle of their body. They wear severely plain clothes from choice. They are really tailor-made men and women. There is little leaning toward any of the softening things in face or form. They are tall rather than plump, sometimes bony like the 1, but ever and always they look strong, dignified, trustworthy. Their clothes are always of good material, and usually the dark shades appeal. The 4 is really the *service* personality—but it has much of strength and helpfulness in its looks and this redeems it from being too plain.

The Negative 4. Very plain, sometimes almost repellant and with severe angles—all emphasized. It is as careless in details as the positive 4 is careful. The negative 4 is useful to the last degree, but lacks artistic touch. They never try to be prepossessing, and they often seem to act as though they are proud of their plainness. They are jealous of beauty and disdainful of popularity, over-worked, and too rigorous with themselves. *Negative* 4 will get up at 4 a.m. because he is so harassed with all he thinks awaits his doing. He will nag and scold if others do not do the same thing. Unnecessarily, he carries the whole world on his shoulders. He resents the fact that others will not do likewise. He doesn't know that he need not do it, and that one who has a 5 vibration will not do it because he is learning the freedom of personal desires. The negative 4 is apt to look hard and strained.

It is difficult to make a *negative* 4 let go of his

authority; and only time and experience will teach him.

WHAT 5 LOOKS LIKE

THE five is very original looking, and "ultra" in every detail. They are in a class by themselves. They have errors of physical angles—curves and angles mixed. Some features are out of proportion, but they are always attractive—always more chic than beautiful. They can wear any sort of extravagant style, with all bright colours. They are always interesting in appearance. An atmosphere of daring permeates them. They are smiling and open in their actions. Their personality is a great factor in their successes.

A negative 5 is extremely bizarre, loud in coloring, startling in style, very irregular in form and features, and extravagant in the use of jewelry. They are showy and unpopular, because the extravagant personality does not win friends.

WHAT 6 LOOKS LIKE

THE positive 6 is comely and attractive, genial and sympathetic looking. It chooses soft colorings and soft, clinging materials. The personality of the 6 is made up of curves, with no obtrusive features. It discards objectionable jewelry, and wears clothes which are always in good taste. Nothing is ultra or bizarre.

They attract greatly by their personality which seems to radiate love and understanding. They are of medium height, usually inclined to plumpness, with rounded shoulders and large hips. They have tender eyes, with a light which says "Come unto me and I will give you rest."

A negative 6 is slouchy—too easy looking. Generally, they wear an inharmonious assortment of clothes, an unsuitable blending of colours. They are careless in detail—indolent in atmosphere and never spick and span. They look ungroomed and unattractive. They make friends, but often fail to succeed because of carelessness; inefficient in action as well as in personality.

WHAT 7 LOOKS LIKE

A POSITIVE 7 looks very much like the positive 1, but more refined and reserved. It chooses neutral colorings, and is often exclusively plain in clothes—the highest type of tailor-made, and always the finest materials. They choose smooth surfaces rather than rough or woollen fabrics. They are painfully neat and unruffled. They have fine hands and feet, and maintain a perfect standard of fitness. They attract the clever and thoughtful, but offend the careless.

A negative 7 is just the opposite of the true type. A careless, unlovely mixing of colours. Coarse clothes, lacking the marks of refinement.

WHAT 8 LOOKS LIKE

A POSITIVE 8 is very attractive. They have all the angles of 1 and 4, with added strength. They are careful in details, and wear plain clothes. They like heavy materials of good quality. They are fond of colours and large jewellery. They love pomp and display, and often cultivate a pompous expression with much ostentation of presence. They cultivate all the things that attract attention. No matter how little money the 8 may have, if his personality symbolizes 8 he will look like a millionaire. The 8 possesses strong powers of attraction. He always turns to those who can step him up in life;

and so he cultivates geniality and is called " Hail fellow well met." He looks capable and executive. Much of an 8's success in life comes through the power personality which 8 uses to advantage.

The negative 8 will lose his power and drop back to the plain, unattractive looks of a 4. They look hard, unloving, and they fail to attract. They look " driven " and inefficient. They drive themselves unmercifully and often become hard unrelenting bosses. They do not attract love because of their severe exterior, although they long for the popularity which the positive type gains through their personality.

They often fail utterly until hard luck kicks them into a bigger effort, and they learn to express through their faces and form the big things which lie latent within them.

WHAT 9 LOOKS LIKE

THE *personality* of a *positive* 9 is beautiful, strong and prepossessing. They keep their looks better than any of the other numbers do. The 3 is second in retaining personality. When the 9 lives rightly they are beautiful unto the grave, years only ripen their loveliness. They have all the beauty of curves. They love harmony in colours rather than contrasts. They turn naturally to the milder things. They are soft, gentle, and have a kindly bearing that attracts all people by their winsome, humanitarian ways. They look like a friend who would lay down his life for his friends.

A negative 9 takes on the character of a negative 3— inharmonious, unfriendly, self-righteous, careless, uncultured and unloving. This is called the number of the *Great Lover*. The *positive* 9 is a true lover. He loves and is beloved in return, but the *negative* 9 finds that he can attract much to himself, and he becomes the libertine and the false lover. He loves approval and will go any length to get it, not only from one but from many. And he seeks to get this in his own way and, finally, he looks slouchy, ill-kept, and degenerate.

WHAT 11 LOOKS LIKE

THE *personality* of 11 is like the 1, *plus*. An 11 is made up of two 1's. They have a refined and spiritual personality. Because of the addition of the other 1 they combine the qualities in form of earth and heaven—of the seen and the unseen. They look inspired, and usually have illumined eyes. They chose the strong and enduring in clothes, but select fine things—smooth materials—like silks and satins. They sometimes gown in smooth, fine velvets, but never in rough, coarse, loud-coloured stuffs. They impress people by their dignified, capable atmosphere. They attract friends through personality, but hold them only when in their souls they are capable and helpful.

The negative 11 lacks spiritual atmosphere, and is loud, unenlightened, and careless. They choose coarse materials in clothes, and ribald colourings. They are conceited and not genial. A negative 11 is a priest astray—the Prodigal Son eating with the swine. He lacks in all the ways that make a positive 11 successful. He loses place, situation, and caste by his torn-down personality.

WHAT 22 LOOKS LIKE

THE *personality* of 22, when it is *positive*, comprises all the sweetness and softness of the 2 plus, and all the power of the 8. They are very strong, of striking appearance and are never passed unnoticed. They look well groomed in any situation, choose the best in clothes and stick to the milder colourings. The 22 loves ostentation and show in jewellery, and is often conspicuous because of this.

The 22 dotes on large things, and nothing small or scrimped appears in their personality. Big, generous-looking and genial, they attract through their general look of efficiency and congeniality.

The negative 22's lose all their power of personality and sink back to the negative 2—and as 2 and 2 equal 4, they fall back to the hardness of the undeveloped 4 and are hard on themselves and on others. They lose their look of geniality and softness, and appear for all the world like a hard boss, or even a bully, hard-faced and cold.

All the double numbers, when *positive*, take on the look and character of the single number plus; but when *negative* they sink lower down in the scale of nothingness than do those of the singles.

SUMMARIZING the personalities of people, the positive numbers look:

1—Distinguished	6—Respectable
2—Approachable	7—Exclusive
3—Attractive	8—Individualized
4—Executive	9—Genial and loving
5—Hospitable	11—Spiritual
	22—Powerful

XLI. SPECIAL NUMBERS

2

THE 2 is often called the first vibration of a liar, because it is not a strong number. It is the number of the great sunshine. When the soul-number is 2 it is hard for the ego to stand firmly; and, when the ego is negative, it is afraid to hold out even for truth. It will lie in fear or for peace at any price.

The 2 is the number of magic. In the first stages of extended vision, the laws of psychometry and necromancy can be used. It is called the heart of " Black Magic " but is also the soul of pure vision and white light 'through pure clairvoyance and cosmovoyance.

3

The 3 is the artistic vibration. It is sometimes called " The Great Pretender." When negative it can bluff, pretend to conceal the true facts and will go to any length to express the personal self.

5

The 5 is the second vibration of a liar. A negative 5 is as full of lies as the negative 2 because he wants to be a popular fellow. He will stretch truth to make his side look victorious and will not hesitate to excuse his personal weaknesses by covering them with false explanations. The 5 stands for sex appetite and self but it also stands for freedom and mastery.

7

The 7 is called "The Sphinx" because the real 7 not only looks but is silent, reserved and timid. It is also wisdom and self-realization. The real 7's motto is, "From the alone to the alone."

9

The 9, when negative, is called the third vibration of a liar. The 9 wants approval. He so instinctively longs to be all things to all men and women that he will exaggerate if it meets his purpose. He must be praised, flattered and approved, or he is wretched. He will move everything in his power, false or true, to exact his ends.

The 9 is called "The Faithless Number" because all other vibrations, 1-2-3-4-5-6-7-8 are included in his vibrations, plus. Everybody loves the 9 for his wisdom and grace. It is natural he should give and take from all. When negative he becomes a ruthless libertine, the lover of all and the husband of none. If he marries anyone but a 9 at heart he is called a flirt, and the lesser vibration suffers from jealousy and neglect. The 9 is more often the pathway of the "broken-hearted" than any other number, although it is also the pathway of divine love and power.

11

The 11 is "The Path of the Penitent" for with its higher vision and power if it falls from its high estate it can reach almost total depravity and suffering. It is symbolized by an "unfrocked priest." It is said, "let him that standeth take heed lest he fall."

22

The 22, when negative, is called "The Black Magician." When power is misused it becomes magic —with a longer arm and a stronger will—to work iniquity. Construction and destruction are born in the soul of the 22. They can well heed, " Choose ye this day whom ye will serve."

The mystics say, " Never judge a man by his work—watch his pleasures."

JUSTICE

If I could dip my pen in living fire,
   And write a message which would never die,
I would write one so full of feeling
   That every heart would answer to its cry.

I would not write of love, or healing—
   I'd leave these themes to others who had time—
But I would pour the pathos of my genius
   Into a plea of justice for mankind.

Justice is man's immortal birthright,
   Whether he be of low or kingly birth;
We all have rights, and in the true adjustment
   There is no high or low upon the earth.
                     —*Julia Seton.*

BOOK THREE
The Psychology of Success

BOOK THREE

BUSINESS PSYCHOLOGY

XLII. THE PLANES OF EXPRESSION

BUSINESS psychology interprets us to ourselves —our relationship to each other, and to things and our environment. When we know this we remember that " God helps those who help themselves."

In order to be successful in any of our undertakings we must be harmoniously related to them through symbol vibrations. The law of *opposites, similars* and *complementaries* obtains in situations and in things as well as in people. There is no use fighting *against* things. There is no need to live a life of demonstration when the frictionless way is the universal way, and effort is never necessary. Effort is the pathway of the unenlightened. Struggle, strain and strife belong to the Novitiate; they have no place in the life or environment of the Enlightened.

Every human being has a country, city, home and occupation ready for him when he is born. Every life has its own commercial value. If it is *set* where it should be it must attract all for which it has power to pay. No one can get anything with nothing to give in exchange. When we get our material of exchange ready and offer it to the Universe it must buy, at the price which we determine. Fame, money and position never find the wrong man. They settle where they are bought and paid for.

All humanity is divided industrially into four divisions of consciousness: Physical, mental, emotional and spiritual. And this gives us our industrial keynote.

When we are in our own industrial place we have a commercial value which our very ability controls. " Man, know thyself!" This is the first commercial commandment. Then we can take our place and ask our own price.

XLIII. POSITIONS FOR VOCATIONS

PHYSICAL VIBRATIONS: 2—5

IF our number-symbols show that most of our vibrations are on the physical side, then we must understand that our commercial value is in the domain of physical work. We must work with our hands. In this division are builders, runners, iron workers, bridge builders, masons, carpenters, plumbers, storekeepers, department workers, sailors, dockyard workers, shipbuilders, drivers, truckmen, painters, interior decorators, explorers, dancers, showmen, theatre builders, screen painters, bookbinders, printers, shipping directors and all positions that call for physical endurance and expression through the instructive senses, without too much detail and technique. This is the field of work for women and men who have emphasized in these symbols of consciousness.

The 5 vibration, being slightly emotional, opens the commercial door to writers, screen painters, entertainers, travelling town managers, caterers, head managers in postal or other Civil Service positions, tobacco merchants, hotel keepers, seaside resort keepers, gamblers and grocers.

The 2 is also able to do psychic work because of his extreme sensitiveness, and may become a diplomat or spy according to his own strength of character.

The 2 or 5 may be a good detective. Women of the 2 vibration are always capable of taking good positions in institutes. They are poor housekeepers, but are kind and understanding, and make good, general workers.

WESTERN SYMBOLOGY

Sometimes a sculptor or modeller has been found with the 2 vibration as his soul number. The 5 is the master explorer.

MENTAL VIBRATIONS 1, 4, 7, 8

THE whole world's work is full of mental opportunities. All natural life calls for reason and mentality. The whole world is built on numbers, and those who can think, plan, reason, calculate, deduce, reckon or relate are in demand everywhere.

The banks, railway offices, clerks, conductors on trams and buses, shipping clerks, stenographers, secretaries, bill clerks, electricians, telephone managers, switchboard operators, accountants, book-keepers, merchants, instrumental musicians, bondsmen recorders, justices of the peace, lawyers, judges—yes, often book-makers and gamblers in stocks—all these and many more positions of accuracy are open to those who know how to find their own line of commercial conquest.

EMOTIONAL VIBRATIONS 3-6-9

THE numbers 3 and 6 are slightly mental, but in life action they are posited on the emotional, and their conquest comes from within, not from without. These are the talkers. It has been said that talk is cheap, but the talk of a 3, 6 and 9 is not cheap when it is devoted to his natural plane of power. Talk is cheap in a machine shop or at an accountant's desk, but it is not cheap as a salesman or as the inspired idealist, the buffer between demand and supply, the mother, the father, the home, the stage, the world itself.

The 3's are entertainers—ever great actors, but joyful, laughing, and full of life. They have hosts of friends, and win easily in any contest for supremacy. They can sing, whistle, dance and work, if the work is light and artistic. They are milliners, drapers, jewellery workers, buyers and sellers, trimmers, architects, illustrators and interior decorators.

The 6's are great home-makers, and all the perfect things of home life are in their hands. They can either keep their own house or another's. They are efficient as musical entertainers in hotels, boarding houses, summer places, and in catering. They are writers and publishers. They take governmental positions, and are able to superintend all positions where tact and skill are required.

People love to hear others talk, and these emotional positions give opportunity for expression. The 3 can only find success where it can be its whole self, unrestrained or unwarped. The whole world wants to be inspired. Only as we keep inspired can we touch life. While we hold our spiritual mastery the world cannot crumble from beneath our feet, and we often need someone outside of ourselves to keep us true to what we feel to be true. The 3's, 6's and 9's are the vibrations that lift us up emotionally and spiritually.

Talking, singing, entertainment and worship have a gigantic commercial value. The world will pay for these while it saves on food. The hunger of the soul is harder to bear than the hunger for bread.

Those who find their vibrations are *positive* in these symbols have many avenues of profit. They have only to offer their genius where it belongs.

SPIRITUAL VIBRATIONS 9-11

THE nine is *emotionally spiritual,* and its field of commercial value is drama, art, opera and humanity. The

WESTERN SYMBOLOGY

9 is the great tragedian, the great lover, the great humanitarian and the universal philanthropist. All universal work—building and inspiring, all lines of musical business, vocal training, singing and acting—are in its hands.

The 9, made up of 3 times 3, is a great comedian. The 9 which is made up of 5 plus 4, may be a fine director, and a 9 made up of 7 plus 2 would be a treasurer, or even a screen painter, under the imagination of 2 and the mind of a 7.

The 9 is the general practitioner in medicine—the great healer. Hospitals, rest homes and sanitoriums are open for his work. He is also a publisher, illustrator, advertising artist, lecturer, writer on humanitarian and religious subjects. He is a good home-builder, but is not domesticated, for he is too universal for personal bondage. ALL the big fee positions of travel and education will welcome 9. Wherever vision, inspiration and efficiency are needed they have value. They do not work well in small places, or with limited people. The 9 is the full measure of being, and it demands big opportunities. Success is the birthright of a 9, but it must seek it along its own psychological association.

The 11 is the hardest vibration to place psychologically, and suffers most when unfitly related. It is the Great High Priest of the Temple, and is kept by the people—or should be if those whose symbol is emphasized live as the vibration indicates. It belongs in the halls of learning and the temples of worship, as healers, consultants, priests, advisors.

All branches of teaching are open to it. It is the true teacher and leader in music, art, literature and religion. This is its field. It errs grievously if it works with its hands. The 11 deals wholly with people and their needs, and is supported by the money of those it serves.

There are also many avenues of commercial value open for writers of books, composers of music, illustrators, singers, lecturers, healers, teachers, masters, leaders of societies and clubs, organizations, schools, founders of new orders and new ideals, higher education, social, financial and religious problems.

The 11 is a non-conformist, a separatist, and does his work best when alone. It is not the success plan for 11 to sink his personality and his ideals in the mass mind of others. He must keep individualized, alone and efficient. Loneliness is good for a creative consciousness. Revelation is not often born fully fledged in a crowd. Thus, 11 means to seek occupation where the " single eye and naked vision " is of value.

When 11 is the weight of our number vibrations, we can only win where we plunge on those things which belong to us. When we do this, we keep the " light burning as a lamp to the feet " of the race. And, in lighting the way for others, we rise with the all; for " He who loses his life shall find it."

COMPOSITE VIBRATION 22

THE twenty-two is *the Great Master Builder*, and with 11 can create a new heaven and a new earth; and with 8 it can keep on building forever. All avenues of life are open. Construction is everywhere and there is always room at the top. All the things of 1-2-3-4-5-6-7-8-9 are open to 22, plus its own master position. It is the head, hands, mind and body of all occupation.

Its vocation is leadership. All the construction of humans invites it—railways, shipbuilding, houses, homes, hospitals, surgeons, churches, cities, roads, dentists, implement makers, moulders, sculptors, electricians, engineers. All that is in *form* is the output of their genius, plus those they direct. There is not a *thing* in human use that is not theirs.

An *idle* 22 is a travesty on business for there is so much room at the top. There are negative people in all these planes who never succeed because they lack the quality or consciousness of success. A *negative* 22 is " jack of all trades but master of none "—hence his bad luck.

The *positive* 22 has the whole world in the hollow of his hand. He can turn anywhere—woman or man. There is no one, save himself, who can say him nay.

SUMMARIZING the planes, let us remember that they are basically physical, mental, emotional and spiritual, with combinations of each. Also, remember that we function through the physical in *instinct,* the mental in *reason,* the emotional in *feeling* and *inspiration,* and the spiritual in *intuition, revelation* and *prophecy.*

All these planes of consciousness are related to vocation. Our business psychology interprets these relationships so that any one who will study his number-symbols will be found to find his lines of least resistance for a life work. There are many square pegs in round holes, and *vice versa;* but this need not be when we find our own line of least resistance, and link up with our own zone of consciousness in our labours.

If the majority of our numbers are physical—2-5—then our commercial value is in accord with the work of this plane. If in the mental—1, 4, 7, 8—then we should hasten to relate ourselves with the things of this plane.

If our symbols show a preponderance of 3-6, then that

is our open door—no man can shut it—for in our own "zone of action" we have the keys of the world's heart, and we are a link between demand and supply.

If we have many numbers of 9 we can turn to humanity to help it in every way. We know that 9 is the magnet which attracts all men to it, and service to man is the highest worship of God.

If it is 11 we have only to hold high our torch of light and join our own great procession that keeps alive the great ideals of love, truth and worship. "They must all be taught of God until God Himself shall be their teacher," and we can find eager hearers everywhere ready to follow and to give as is given unto them. We must steadily talk and teach of God, even in a seemingly Godless world, until men, seeing, shall take heart again.

The 22 has the world at its back. If we fail it is because we are spiritual slackers on all planes; for to whom much is given, much is required.

XLIV. NUMBER COMBINATIONS IN BUSINESS

In combinations for business success there is a deep psychological law at work, which, if overlooked, brings disaster.

Business concerns must be combined with directors and managers under the law of opposites in number symbols. To have *four* men *who are alike in number symbols* means that only *one* man will be on the job. They will think too much alike to discern all the angles of the business. To put a physical man in a mental man's place is to court failure; and to put an emotional or spiritual man in a physical or mental department is foolhardiness. Each department in a home, store, business or office also has its own *four* planes of consciousness. Anyone who is wise will fill them appropriately.

If a business psychologist were permitted to investigate the setting of half the business houses in any city and to re-arrange the departments, or to fill the departments with clerks of the quality of consciousness needed, the next month's receipts would justify his wisdom. In one of the big stores in a large city there was a "lagging behind" in the sales of the jewelry department. The head manager asked me to look into the cause, and to find if it lay in the quality of the salesmanship. Investigation in the department disclosed the fact that all the saleswomen were on the physical—emotional plane—and had no real affinity for the department.

Later I was in the music department in search of some banjo music, and found several mental clerks who knew very little about any of the stock—and cared less. They were thinkers, not feelers. I told the manager where the fault lay. No one cares to have a saleswoman singing to herself while she sells jewelry, as his clerks did. However, when he goes to the music stall he is glad of an opportunity to find one who can sing. There was nothing the matter with the departments of jewelry and music—except that the saleswomen of each were in the wrong place.

Business psychology is no myth. The truly efficient business houses of to-day have discovered this. They rearrange their sales personnel to fit their needs.

In an elevator in one of the large cities, I heard the rather fine looking elevator man always humming the latest opera or the latest song-hit of the city. One day I said to him, " You ought to be in a minstrel show instead of shooting a lift," and he replied, " I never thought of that, but I wish I might. I hate this."

I asked the principal of a music school to take him in and to prepare him for the singing world. He did, and, within a year, I had the pleasure of hearing him " put over " a more than acceptable repertoire, and discovered that he was going straight to the top in the singing world.

There's no need putting up with what is not good enough, and the reason can nearly always be found in the misfit application. We never do our best save in the things that really belong to our type, and it is wasted effort to drive ourselves on, along lines of uncongenial work.

Since we know that there is a place and a work and a pay for everyone, we should seek until we find our line of least resistance and our highest commercial value. Our number vibrations reveal this. What to do for a life work is not difficult to discover when once we determine the plane of expression in which we have *power*.

Were we starting a farm, we would not go among preachers or artists for our labourers. We would look for physical, emotional and mental help. Were we buying an investment, we would not ask the advice of farmers or religionists. We would go to *mental* minds —those who calculate and relate. If our investment is a business we will win greatly by giving every department its own kind of workers. If we were painting a picture or sculpturing a statue we would not accept the advice of a purely physical or mental man for our ideal or concepts. If we were uncertain about form, detail or outline, only these thinkers, 1-4-8-22, would do. They should be able to put us right at once.

Were we to open a religious work we would not expect to win with an army of unconverted workers. We would expect success to follow true religious zeal and ardour, and the religious body to grow in ideality, inspiration and revelation. Only those whose souls were anchored in the white light of consecration and service would perform such work efficiently enough to bring success. Spiritual work calls for religionists.

If we were in a bank, at an accountant's desk, or in a scientist's laboratory—a true mentalist—we would not expect to get on easily with a singing, noisy, temperamental emotionalist. Silence is golden in the ranks of clerical business, and any wasted effort brings indifferent success.

If we were in the song, dance and sunshine of perfected self-expression—entertaining and inspiring—we would not want a cold mentalist as our associate. Vaudeville stunts often fail simply because, as a business venture, they are not *psychologically accurate.*

A church needs the message and the messenger. It also needs the worker, the law-giver and treasurer. These are the outer priests who keep and build the temple; but they will fail at the altar or Sacrament Table, and they cannot be Keeper of the Inner Shrine. Neither can the one whose consciousness is attuned to do this thing build the temple or watch its supply. A mystic demands (and should have) a correlative environment. It is only a city which is filled with physical, mental materialists, or spiritual slackers that stones its prophets.

In running a restaurant we need to fit out our establishment from the dishwashers to the head-waiter. We would fail of success if we gave the head-waiter's place to the dishwasher. The dishwasher must be physical, while the head-waiter must be physical, emotional, genial, and at one with the crowd.

The 1-4-8 are buyers, 3-6-9 waitresses, 11-3-9 harpists, violinists, soloists, and decorators, 4-7-8 instrumental musicians, 4 builders, 7 cashiers and 8 directors.

When a restaurant, hotel or business of any kind is managed by those who instinctively know their part and can do it, success must begin and it will continue permanently.

There are *negatives* in every number, and all business suffers from these. They are driftwood or ciphers in the big human equation. A negative person must be taught to understand his weaknesses, also to use the strength of his character. Often wonderful workers and successes can be produced from seemingly very green and inferior characters.

If we desire our business to reach its fullest efficiency, we must begin with the consciousness which we have in stock. All other stock will decay on the shelves unless we have some more of the same kind in head, heart and hand. " Business misfits " are a reality. The business builders have suffered long and been kind. However, workers nowadays must learn that there is very little chance for the dull ones who clog the market with less than half their consciousness on tap. Business is rapidly passing into the hands of the aware—the efficient—those who know themselves and their capacity, and can deliver the goods.

Life always pays for life. It pays to-day, to-morrow and forever. Life is a repository, and what we put in we must take out. We cannot put one hundred per cent. of ourselves into the syllabus where we are unfit. Only where our treasures are, will our hearts be. The 4 will never find true delight in the successes of 9, or *vice versa*. An 11 will detest the life and successes of 3 or 8. The 3 or 8 will pine away and grow dull by always living in the atmosphere of 9 or 11.

It was never intended that we should give all our genius and strength to help others grow great in their own way. Our souls naturally demand their own satisfaction. We long to have more of our substance, so, after a while, we naturally reject another fellow's job. Not that we mean to do so, but it never can call out from us all that pent-up zeal we would display in working with, where, and what we like.

To prosper, business must be four square—mind, body, soul and spirit—and these forces are kept alive only by the people who have these powers. A home cannot be all mental, physical, emotional or spiritual and persist as a home. It must comfort all its inhabitants, and as soon as one quality of consciousness dominates it is no longer a home, but a prison.

Many men of many minds, so combined as to make the One Mind in all through all,—*this is business psychology*. This is success—from the peanut stand on the corner to the highest official offices in the world.

XLV. YOUR NUMBERS AND YOUR VOCATIONS

1

LEADERSHIP belongs to the 1. They are editors, writers, advertisers, overseers, heads of business concerns, department managers, bank managers, bank clerks, office clerks, railroad managers or directors, heads of institutions or organizations, consulting lawyers, surgeons, dressmakers, master builders, contractors, community leaders, presidents of lodges or societies, etc., etc.

The 1 should always keep a place of individual leadership and authority. He does better alone than when his work is mixed in others' affairs, or he is subordinated. He should lead rather than follow. These delineations apply both to men and to women.

2

THE 2's are good mixers, and should work with others. They are co-operation workers, singers, artists, office workers, hotel workers, cooks, companions, nurses, waiters, salesmen of groceries and other materials, florists, railroad conductors, tramway men, workers in large associations, bus drivers, interior decorators, gardeners, storekeepers, millinery makers, or workers with machines in dressmaking establishments, caretakers, etc., etc.

The 2 should always work with others. He succeeds better in association than with individual projects. The

2 is too gentle to be strongly initiative. The 2 is often a healer and clairvoyant.

3

THE 3 is a musician, vocal or instrumental, an entertainer, lecturer, salesman, traveller, buyer, actor, stage manager, comedian or lighter tragedy, writer, illustrator, demonstrator, entertainer for hotels or summer resorts, band organizer and leader, good industrial salesman, or of stocks and bonds, agriculturist, jeweller, milliner, club hostess, general practitioner in medicine, welfare worker, church choir leader, missionary, etc., etc.

The 3 can readily work alone or with others. Success depends on the 3's careful selection and application. The 3 is a scattering number.

4

THE 4 is an organizer, manager, lodge keeper, band leader, musician, instrumental or vocal, composer, author, advertisement writer and illustrator, bank manager, business psychologist, clerk, stenographer, school teacher, dressmaker, shop keeper, hardware salesman, billing and shipping clerk, accountant, treasurer and auditor, recorder, industrial inventor, juryman, specialist in medicine, minor surgery, astrologist, scientist, druggist, farm director, etc., etc.

The 4 is a hard worker and a born organizer. His work is to organize for everybody, and to keep the control of the organization in his own hands. He can always build up what is torn down.

5

THE 5 is a travelling salesman, and can sell anything that interests him. He is also an explorer, miner, or promoter, could be a specialist in diamond mines or money interests. The 5 is an international representative, congressman, president of lodges, associations and societies, engineering expert, civil servant, nurse, hospital manager, college expert, college professor, park commissioner, policeman, detective, criminal lawyer, theatre manager, dramatic critic.

The 5 is all things to all men, and his power is in association with his own desires. He fails under repression.

6

THE 6 is the homemaker, the builder, the keeper, miner, postal clerk, dramatic artist, vocalist, writer, painter, architect, real estate dealer, salesman for all home necessities, piano builder, furniture dealer in antiques, grocer, carpenter, gardener, florist, fruit grower or dealer, farmer, cattle man, hotel keeper, institutional worker or manager, milliner, nurse, hospital superintendent, etc., etc.

The 6 works best when in combination with others. He can follow better than he can lead. In any but in his own domain he is apt to lack initiative.

7

THE 7 is a law giver, judge, lawyer, accountant, bookkeeper, writer, recorder, auditor, bank manager or clerk, shipping clerk, translation expert, steamship manager, stenographer, instrumental musician, band director, choir leader, architect, master weaver, shop director, steel worker and manager, reporter of general news, baseball umpire, concert manager, manager of tourist bureau, travelling manager, state director, minister of government, director in schools and universities.

There is no line of executive work closed to a 7. He is calm and steady, an executive, a master of details, and a past master in managing.

8

THE 8 is the head of the world—an organizer and a leader, executive and director, newspaper owner, land owner, home owner, ship owner and builder, master carpenter, railroad owner, institution builder, head of corporations, big investor, promoter, international politician, and a financier.

The 8 makes a success of anything material. Should be an employer rather than an employee. The 8 can live by the brain and brawn of his fellowmen. The 8 starts the things which others finish. He is the master organizer, leader, instructor, director, the head of all big associations, a ruler of finance. He always wins if he tries.

9

THE 9 is an editor, publisher, reporter, singer, entertainer, higher educationalist, travelling evangelist, master salesman, head of all welfare and religious organizations, juryman, hotel keeper, seaside resort manager, organizer of concerts, interior decorator, painter, composer, landscape gardener, agriculturist, specialist in the growing of fruits and flowers, head of humanitarian movements, minister, missionary, hospital director, nurse, general practitioner in medicine, milliner, florist, confectioner, draper, window dresser, manager of an institution, etc., etc.

The 9 is successful in any department of life that needs kindness and inspiration.

11

THE 11 is the evangelist, actor, impersonator, illustrator, architect, interior decorator, travelling buyer, silk merchant, diamond salesman, jeweller, religious writer, street evangelist and singer, minister, church housekeeper, doctor, healer, lecturer, resident priest, consultant, judge, welfare and charity organization worker.

Any work that has to do with spiritual betterment belongs to the 11. The 11 should work with ideals rather than with things. He belongs to the people and should always serve them in some spiritual capacity.

22

THE 22 is the great overlord. He directs all others. His field is with transportation at home or abroad, building, shipping, buying, and the publication of newspapers, magazines and books. His work is planning cities, opening up new territories, landscaping railroads, suburbs, a builder and planner of hospitals, churches, homes, museums, etc., etc. He is the negotiator for international combinations, the director of telegraph, or radio communication, government supplies, or army and navy affairs. He is prime minister or president of all concerns—even of nations.

The 22 is the power position, and when a 22 has developed his consciousness to fit his number symbol he can ask whatsoever he will. Nothing will be impossible unto him. These vocations hold good for both men and women. Opportunity never plays favourites, but it delivers to those who can produce the qualities that win.

XLVI. "LUCKY," OR CONSTRUCTIVE, NUMBERS

LIFE always pays in full—being for being in perfect part. If we sow to the wind we reap the whirlwind. If we sow to joy, happiness, success, freedom and peace we get the fruits of our sowing. Just as there are symbol vibrations which challenge our progress and bring us our negative reactions, so there are also symbol vibrations which bring to us our best.

There are many people whom the world calls lucky. Everything they touch prospers. Many are born rich, healthy, beautiful and wise. Unless we know the higher laws we will drift on in wonder and speculation about them.

There are certain number symbols which reveal the story. If we know these we may read the riddle of success and good fortune.

There are *six power positions,* and these " lucky " people have one or more of them. That is the reason they are what we call fortunate. *The number vibrations of power positions are:* 2-5-7-8-9-11-22. These symbolize the qualities of consciousness which are necessary to control, to attract and to direct life.

If we were to build a man with a perfect quality of consciousness we would presuppose that he was an individual, that he knew his own soul, and had started out to develop himself along higher lines of conquest. He would, in well marked degrees, need to include, positively, the qualities of 2-5-7-8-9-11-22 before he would become a magnet attracting to himself ALL the good things life has ready to provide. Everyone gets

WESTERN SYMBOLOGY

some things; but only the master gets *all*.

THE 2 is the vibration of sensitiveness, and the first vibrations of a master is awareness and alertness in the physical. He must see, hear, taste, smell and sense, so that where others feel nothing, he can feel vibrations of thought and action. The 2 must be instinctively alert, and instinct is the first quality to step up. This power to sense things instinctively and register in extended sign, hearing, taste, touch and smell, puts him ahead of the multitude, who, having eyes, see not, and having ears, hear not. With all these senses stepped up he becomes a mystic, a diplomat, a revelator, and he can soft pedal wherever life is hard.

A *positive* 2 is the first step on the path to power. As he unfolds he comes to clairvoyance, clairaudience and psychic extension and can increase his human sensibilities by the wisdom behind the veils. The positive 2 is all things to all men, and can enter into everyone's interests better than any other number. He is able to sink himself; and, through this, he wins popularity and opportunity. His friends assist him to his heart's desire. Because of this he is called lucky.

THE 5 is the next vibration of power. A master of men must be free, unbound by faction or by creed. He must be able to look and to reason with unbiased judgment (mind), and be able to cut loose from that which limits his progress. He must let the dead past bury its dead, and press on to the new. A *positive* 5 is a master, because he can do as he pleases, yet he never pleases to do anything but that which is best for himself and others. He is good, but not sanctimonious. He is in the world, and at the same time he is free to investigate heaven.

The 5 is the number of self-mastery, and he who conquers himself is fitted to lead the race and to attract to himself all that is best and wisely dispense it. The 5 is a good steward for life's generosity.

THE 7 is the next power number vibration. It includes the power to keep still. No one who babbles will ever come into the sanctuary or to the seats of great power. There are many souls in the world who must have a confessional, for there are sorrows born of human error which are too heavy to be borne alone. The 7 is a confessional for those who must tell their woes—a repository for secrets. It is written, " Two men can keep a secret when one of them is dead," but a *positive* 7 can keep a secret living or dead. It is his vocation. With the advice of a 7, humanity often saves itself.

The 7 has buried his sorrow—hence he is able to help with the world's share. The strong, deep, pure stream of silent consciousness comforts, heals, blesses, and gives to the world the best he knows. And the world gives back to him.

THE 8 is the next vibration. The 8 is power, name, place, and the 8 can lead, construct, and direct. All the world falls into line with the man that declares himself a master, and a positive 8 is the quality of consciousness, of mastery, wealth and power.

It is a great thing to be able to make situations for ourselves; but it is far greater to *plus* this with the ability to make situations for others also. This is to furnish a soil in which other lives can grow great. The 8 works with things first, and people second. He can create, evolve, unfold and distribute, as well as help others to do the same. His very efficiency brings universal opportunity. His skilled consciousness has no competition. His capacity is the pivot of his power and success.

THE 9 is the next in the path of power. This means love. Love to God—love to man—love to self. Without love, men could not grow. It is love, not hate, that leads the race up to supreme heights.

The 9 is *the great lover.* It is forgiveness and a new chance. " Old things pass away and are remembered not again." The 9 is the great healer, for love heals. The 9 is the great sympathizer. His power is with *people;* not with things. In the atmosphere of a *positive* 9 the weak feel the great invitation, " Come unto me, and I will give you rest." Their success comes through the universal trust they establish in the minds of others. They are close enough to God not to be mistaken, and too close to humanity to be misunderstood. They give much, and to them much is given.

THE 11 is the vibration of reverence and worship. It is the message, the messenger, and the temple. Its symbol is the church steeple which says silently, " Remember God."

Some people live too close to earth to feel reverence. They have no shrines and would destroy ours, or drive the beasts of the fields into our temples. Nothing ever moves them out of the commonplace, but the 11 has thoughts that turn upward.

The 11 is the vibration of home, mother, love, heaven and other great sensations. It is like the sound of a heavenly organ in a grand " Amen,"—like the hush of the mountains, the beat of the surf on the empty shores, the whirr of the bird wings over the trees, the springing of the grass, the opening of a flower. Although too subtle to analyze, it is that wonderful something that lifts all life out of the commonplace, the pretty, the little, and the nice, and makes it great, tremendous, splendid.

The 11 is the double 1, earth and heaven joined—and its success and power come from being able to make the plainest places half-divine by giving life everywhere a glory not its own. It is thus the 11 keeps the hearts and souls of men looking upward. Humanity seeks what it does not have in itself. *To get* is the keynote of race progress. *To have* is the mystics' answer!

THE 22 is the *outer form* of all things. It is the master-builder that brings all life into one great body—mind, soul, and spirit. The 22 finishes all that others have begun. Without 22 the world would have no respite. The 22 builds with greater pause when life puts on the last hinges of the human house. The 22 builds for all. This quality of consciousness gives us universities, hospitals, depots, railroads, steamships, hotels, institutions, newspapers, books, music, sculptoring, gigantic canvases. " So carried Pericles the woman that he loved." Thus, centuries after, humanity could worship his great genius. Creative genius works out in strong enduring forms, such as the temples of Karnak —Luxor—Rome—Pompeii. Great things have chronicled the qualities of these messengers.

When all the best that life can produce lies hidden in the deep recesses of their mind, it is not strange that 22 has the world in the hollow of his hand.

A *positive* 22 can say " Let there be light," and there will be the light of a higher civilization everywhere. Here a bridge, there an iron railway, yonder great piles of bricks and mortar, will tell through the centuries of his skill. Gigantic statues and stately columns stand to tell of the power position 22 won by just living 100 per cent. the thing it is in reality.

The 2-5-7-8-9-11 and 22—these are the vibrations of mastery. We may have one or more in our name and numbers. Each one is worth to us just what it represents. We are wise if we know how to plunge forward realizing what it all means.

> 2. Sensitiveness—vision—diplomacy.
> 5. Freedom and self-mastery.
> 7. Silence and meditation—strength.
> 9. Love—understanding—humanity.
> 11. Reverence—worship—revelation.
> 22. Genius—organization—usefulness.

TOGETHER these form an eternal armour for success at the crest of life. This is luck, not by accident, but by slow self-conquest and comradeship with the experiences that develop these qualities in our soul. When we have these we are, in truth, " The darling of the gods." We are a " Lucky fellow "—but we bought them with the price of our own self—and the price was " paid down."

The question is asked: Where must these numbers be in the symbology to give us their power? Let me repeat: They may be anywhere in the name, initiation, personality, vocation, soul, or in the digits of our divisions. The main questions to ask are: How many of these number-symbols appear in my equation? What are they? How many are of the same kind? Then, remembering that, one and all, they stand for a definite good, it is not hard to discover which ones of the number make up your name. Knowing this and emphasizing the qualities of consciousness which they indicate—they become the mascot by which we win.

XLVII. "UNLUCKY," OR RECONSTRUCTIVE NUMBERS

THERE is no such thing as "lucky" or "unlucky"—but the race-mind believes in these things and does not know the reason why.

There is only one intelligence in the Universe, but there are two distinct actions on the Intelligence. One that builds up and holds together—always going on in fresh creation. The other tears down, pulls apart and breaks up—so that all things can be reconstructed or reformed. Both actions are good. They are twin born. At their center lies the eternal law of poise and progress. What humanity calls "lucky" or "unlucky" is simply the action of these two forces.

When all things work harmoniously, and health, wealth and success follow every action, then we say we are "lucky"—that we are "on the knees of the gods," "We have been born with a silver spoon in our mouth," or "He is a lucky chap."

But when one thing after another fails—when life is one of loss rather than gain—when change, decay and despair come as a result of all we do, or all we see in the life of another, then we say, "Poor unlucky Devil!" "It's hard luck!" "He was born unlucky," "The fates are against him," or the expression, "One cannot war with the stars."

Luck is simply the evidence of atonement (at-one-ment) with universal harmony. It is evidence that our own vibrations are in tune with the Infinite One—that our thoughts, words and deeds are constructive; not reconstructive.

XLVIII. ELEMENTAL FORCES

It is useless to deny that there are universal potencies for reconstruction. We must understand this—or fall.

There are only five elements, as we have learned,—Light, Air, Fire, Water, Earth. Each of these has a constructive and reconstructive force; and man and his environment are of this universal stuff.

Light makes the world fit to live in, yet too much light can blind. The ether transformed into air gives the breath of the Almighty that giveth us life. However, too much air can become a tornado and wreck a whole country.

Fire warms and blesses us, and fits the planet for habitation. Yet, in it lies the power to lay whole cities into heaps of white ashes. Earth is the foundation of all that moves and has beauty. With it under our feet we feel heroic. But one little slip or shiver, and beauty, greatness and power lies in shattered ruins everywhere.

All these powers localize in us. We have in us the calm light of reason and revelation; the changing tender emotions of the air; the warm, loving impulses of the sun and the fire; the shifting desires and reflections of the water and the sun and fire—and the certain solid and enduring qualities of the earth. But we have also the reconstructive qualities, the blindness of physical, mental and spiritual vision which will not reason or see light; the fearful tornadoes of destructive emotions; the burning and lustful passions of the fire; the unstability of character, which is as unstable as the water, and sometimes, a soul's stagnation when the waves of our own misery beat upon us. And, again, we have the violent quakes of earth, when in some mad hour our own foolishness engulfs us.

There is this reconstructive and constructive quality in every kingdom. The mineral has its gold and silver as well as its poisonous metals. The vegetable kingdom holds the deadly nightshade as well as the violet and the rose. The animal kingdom has the fatal cobra as well as the gentle dove.

The kingdom of man has its human devils who live in darkness and love the things of darkness better than they love the things of light. They plunder, rape, kill, lie, cheat and steal. All this they do in a world where walk beside them those who keep the commandments, and who are wholly constructive.

All these qualities of reconstructive consciousness are ours because we attracted them to us with our own desires, our hate, our fear, worry, resistance, condemnation, criticism, resentment, envy, lust, greed, dishonesty, licentiousness, slothfulness, drunkenness, revenge, lying, stealing, cheating, profiteering, bragging, domineering, and many other offences which link the soul of man with the kingdom of reconstructives, of " Bad Luck."

" We become the reaper of the things we sow—the sesame brings sesame and the corn brings corn." These qualities of consciousness are poisonous metals, the deadly nightshade, the fatal cobra, the devils of our life. Through these unregenerate qualities we reap our bad luck, our hard times—our own balance sheet. By them we learn that " the way of the transgressor is hard." By studying over our number symbols we learn over what line of malefaction we have opened the door to the things that we do not want.

XLIX. THE MALEFIC SYMBOLS

THESE states of consciousness are symbolized by the numbers 14, 16 and 19. No matter where these occur, in the personality, soul, destiny or initiation, they tell the story of where to expect reconstruction.

14

THE 14 is the great destroyer, and expresses its power on the physical plane. It brings bitter changes, loss, sickness, sudden deaths, and sometimes deformities. It is a token of lack of balance in the physical things of life. A hunchback with a 14 shows too much saturation of physical appetites. In personality it indicates too much clinging to the physical sensations of life. If 14 is the soul number it means interrupted love and interruption in all emotional affairs. If 14 is in the destiny it suggests that there is a chance for disappointed hopes and a new balancing of forces.

If 14 is in the initiation it is a lesson to be learned— to have and to hold, then let go, and still to stand victorious in soul. When one can pass it to the digit 5 one finds freedom and peace; for surely when the last thing has been taken away the soul is free, and it can say " I triumph still."

The 14 has most to do on the physical plane. If personality is made up of 14, we can be sure that he will have errors of physical angles and show his destructive past in his own form. The 14 is a big vibration to conquer, for it takes so much away—always making for new adventures in friends, business and homes. People often wonder at this law of loss and change in their life—never understanding that their own vibrations brought it forth.

But when once we know we can never *not* know; and when we find we must *let* go, we learn to open our hands and to push. The one who gets through and lets go constructively and not with tears, pain or grief, has the happiest ending. After all, he finds that life never takes one thing away without giving something else. When he *loves* the law of change he has *conquered* change itself.

16

THE 16 is the " falling tower." The ancients said it was the symbol of a man falling from a high tower with his crown in his hand. It symbolized humiliation, harassment of spirit, unfortunate love affairs, unhappy marriages and discontent in life. In the personality number it means humiliation in physical things, loss of name, place, power, position, even fortunes, false investments, to be led up to high positions and then to be suddenly turned down.

If 16 is in the soul vibration it means broken dreams —sometimes a broken heart—false friendships, mis-alliances, stooping to conquer, vexations of spirit, perplexities, unwanted, disappointments in children, parents and lovers.

The 16 is the number of faithless, faulty loving, of broken promises, of gaining love in some unholy way and then playing false to it. The 16 in soul will learn to his full understanding the truth Edwin Markham taught:

" One thing shines clear in the world's sweet reason—
  One lightning o'er the chasm runs;
 That to turn from Love is the world's one treason—
  And treads down all the suns."

At last the 16 learns not to traffic in hearts; not to take gifts of love he does not return. He learns that life does not mean that one is to give and another to receive, but that the universal law says, " Being for being in perfect part—soul for a soul—life for a life, and a heart for a faithful heart."

The 16 is not wholly an unfriendly number, but it is a really painful one for anyone to transmute. Where it can be poised in its digit (1 plus 6 equals 7) it becomes a vibration of peace and rest. In silence and meditation is its strength. The 7 is the number of the mystic. When one goes within and rests on the spirit he is no longer torn by trifles of the outer world. The indwelling sense of the Spirit—his own spirit linked with the universal—is the goal of 16. Thus, the Kingdom of Heaven within us can be made manifest.

If 16 is in the initiation number, then all the tragedies of the falling tower must be learned. We will rise to fall again, love to lose, hold to let go, have and have not. Often our hearts will be dragged out to slaughter. When we have given our all we will often feel that there is no one to give to us. But, clinging to the qualities of consciousness of transmuting 16 to 7, our path becomes tranquil. Whenever we have learned the lessons of 16 and have passed it to the digit 7, it is written, " He has won a heart of gold for all eternity, and entered into the true Rest."

19

THE other reconstructive number is the 19. It is called " The Collector of Customs," for this number vibration means that we will pay in full. It is the endurance vibration, or the number of a test incarnation.

It brings everything to a focus, winds up old Karmic accounts and starts anew.

If 19 is in the physical there will come all kinds of physical tests of endurance. Only when we can do ten times more physically than anyone around us, and do it uncomplainingly, have we won. How much can we stand? The 19 makes us learn to stand all that our highest desires demand. If our desires call for strong physical endurance, then 19 sets the situation from which we cannot escape until we have paid in full measure, pressed down and running over.

When 19 is in the soul vibration our test will be with both life and death. The 19 leads us to the edge of the grave and teaches us to look across death to life, and from loss to gain. Our hearts are tried until we can merge all our consciousness into the 10 or the 1 plus; and, looking neither backward nor forward, just walk on—letting life do its best or its worst. The ancients called 19 " the vibration of surrender," for it is in this that we learn to link our life with the universal life, and, losing our life we find it on the tablelands of Higher Desires.

The 19 learns to say:

" Oh life, take all you ever gave!
   Strew with despair my pathway, round about!
I'll open e'en the darkness of the grave,
   And let the secrets of the past come out! "

With 19 in the soul, no secrets rest with us alone. Life drags everything out into the light. Don't tell your secret to 19, for it is written " The angels will hear and tell God." This means simply that all life will find it out. The 19 cannot hide anywhere, and it can not live to itself. Publicity is its crucifixion—until it puts all of its cards of life face upwards.

If 19 is in the destiny, then it is surely the Olympic Race. It may reach its destiny stripped of everything, but its reward will come if it holds on at each pause—even when there is nothing left but the power within that says, "*Hold on!*"

The 19 in the initiation is just some more of the same thing. Sometimes the indolent souls and minds of men hate to face the facts of their own desires. They hope to gain heaven on flowery beds of ease. But life doesn't reckon that way. And " eye for an eye " on the physical plane. " With what measure ye mete, it shall be meted out to you " on the soul plane. And, " whatsoever ye sow, ye reap " on the path of initiation. And destiny says " We shall come rejoicing, bringing in the sheaves."

So 19 on initiation brings to us what we have sown in desires. " Not one jot or tittle of the law will pass away." We must pay in full everywhere. We must put in what we want to take out. What we have taken out and have not paid for, must be paid for now. Sometimes our accounts are closely balanced and our payments seem easy, but usually we struggle with the burdens of our past. Old people, old situations, old things bind us. We are bound when we would be free. The 19 teaches us not to ask of life any more than we wish to pay. It is not possible to get something for nothing, and if we take things this way, 19 will collect its customs, and " When the law cometh what will we say to it, and when it questioneth, what will be answer?"

When we understand we will not bother or resist, but pay quickly, and pay everywhere. We pay with our time, money and ourselves, but after a while we do get paid up, and pass on to 10, where we are ready to start anew, plus the wisdom we have won in the universal settling of our debts.

It's no use being sentimental, fearful, or doubtful about these malefic number vibrations. They are as certain as day and night, or as heat and cold. Men did not make them. They are universally existent. However, in their manner of thinking, speaking and acting men set vibrations in motion which link them with these unwholesome experiences; and about which they repine in ignorance.

The 14, 16 and 19 are the great reconstructions—destroying so that man may create with the new soul of 5, 7 or 10—the power of construction, freedom, rest, and perfected individuality. All these can help us to meet our fate—or our unlucky stars, or our unhappy experiences. And, as we draw from them their essence we are able to replace with love, worship and service until the universal law brings to us the vibrations of power only.

The 14, 16 and 19 are only ourselves. We need not fear our own creations. It may be mile after mile of the dark—but after the last mile it is day. Or, if it is not day, it is that thin dawn, within the breast, which the slayer himself can slay and clear the atmosphere.

The 13 has often been looked upon by some as an unlucky number, but it is not really. We must remember the component parts of 13. We find it is composed of 1 and 3, which reduced to a digit is 4. We must read the meaning of 1, 3, and 4 in vocation, soul, personality, destiny and ruling passion. We will then understand all their possibilities.

The 13 has in it all the power of a great individuality, both positive and negative—the power of perfected personal expression, and the power of skillful organization. Whenever these vibrations are lived constructively they give great possibilities and opportunities therefor. The ancients considered this one of the most fortunate, as well as one of the most unfortunate numbers, because the powers of life and death are in the scope of its vibrations. When we are tremendously individualized and self-efficient it is sometimes hard to have patience with dullards and weaklings. Nevertheless, 13, on account of its totality of 4, demands service to others. And it is service not only in our own way, but in the way which we can best serve them. The 13 always means the opportunity to do big things with the many. It is not a number of isolation. It has in itself the tendencies of great selfishness, self-righteousness and brutal mastery. It is a hard vibration for the undeveloped to live graciously. Any violation of its greater laws will lay the lash of correction on our life. But, lived positively, the 13 brings the very highest fame, publicity, and glory.

L. HOW AND WHEN TO CHANGE A NAME

WE should know the names which bring to us the vibrations of the things we desire. If we are in art, we should have an artistic number symbol; if in drama, dramatic symbols; if domestic, domestic vibrations, etc., etc. One doesn't take a dramatic number symbol if he wants to be a farmer; or a farmer vibration if he wants to be a banker. He should have the natural vibration of that which he wishes to be.

So many people do not know that their *entering* and *closing* vibrations are their test vibrations. Instead of simply laying down their load and using only the number symbols that will help them to rise like a kite or an unloaded balloon, they try to drag along in the vibrations of some of the lesser symbols.

Again, sometimes we have *mixed* vibrations in our names. We have one name made up almost wholly of numbers of the *inside*, 1-3-5-7, and another one made up wholly of numbers of the *outside*, 2-4-6-8-22. These bring great conflict and great power, but there are few who fully accomplish themselves in both in one life; and, a still more limited number ever know the reason why they do not reach that point of accomplishment.

The change should depend upon the balance of power within the names. If the inside numbers are more, and their value is higher than those of the outside numbers, then all of the other names should be given up, and *vice versa*. If the outside numbers, 2-4-6-8-22, have the balance of power, then the inside numbers, 1-3-5-7, should be laid down and all consciousness given over to these symbols and their attraction. Sometimes we can determine this for ourselves, through our own soul's desire; and can easily choose the things of our master vibration, because they are the things of our highest desires.

When we rid ourselves of conflicting vibrations in our own name we will find that life changes for us. We are free to stay free, because we are one with life's finer forces.

We do not lose the qualities of consciousness of all the names we discontinue. No indeed! However, we relegate them to a place of impotency and take their experiences in a neutral manner. They no longer have the power to control or to object. They are swept along in the stronger stream of our new vibrations. If we had a crippled foot or hand we would not attempt to do our life's best work with it. We would put it aside and put forward our normal limb to carry us onward. Our number symbols should be used in a like manner. Some of these are weak; others are strong. Some are in concord; others are in discord. We need not strike a discord unless we want to do so. John Smith " in shorts ' is still John Smith when he is in a dress suit—only expressed differently.

Because we have struck inharmonious vibrations in our past, it is no sign that we must continue to do so. The master is always ready when the student is. Just as soon as we know, we can change our tune.

Someone said, " I was born poor." We say, " Yes, of course "—because that is the symbol of your old qualities of consciousness; and the output of the laws you set in motion for yourself. But by the great cosmic laws of increasing purposes you were not born to stay poor. We were not born to stay ill, or unhappy, or unsuccessful,—for " In my Father's house are many mansions." However, we are obliged to build the ladder by which we climb past our dead self to higher things.

We must not think that any number symbols are bad. They are not. All numbers and names are good —perfect for the thing that they symbolize. One who wishes to be master of all material things would not have an easy time accomplishing this if he had the majority of his symbols in *inside* receptive numbers, 1-3-5-7-9-11.

There are combinations of number symbols that work disaster to those who do not know the eternal law, and who cannot dominate their lesser vibrations. Opium in the hands of a skilled physician becomes a constructive thing and subdues pain. In the hands of an ignorant person opium would numb or destroy. Just so with these symbols of life which we write for ourselves and then permit *them* to master us—not because we must, but because we are not masters of our own symbology.

There are number symbols for every degree of human consciousness. If we know how we can choose in each incarnation not only to finish what we brought with us, but so skillfully to select the next step of our unfoldment that we can say, " I know from whence I come and whither I go."

We come in " the reaper of the things we sowed," and we go out the reaper of the things we sow here and now. What we build in *time* we take with us into Eternity. We are in Eternity *now*. This moment we are in time. We can choose this day what we will serve. And, forcing the old to take on the colour of the new, we begin rebuilding. We cannot put new wine into old bottles, but we canthrow away the old wine if it is worthless; and, seeking a new vineyard, we can gather new grapes for a better wine.

We must have the name we were given because we gave it to ourselves in universal cosmic law. We named, numbered, chorded and placed ourselves for our plunge into the pool of life. Sometime we must come to the top again, and swim to a new shore. *Why not now?* New names bring new vibrations, new vibrations bring new worlds of consciousness, and a new consciousness brings new situations, people and things. A new horizon brings a new splendour.

Remember there are no unlucky names or numbers. They are just letters and numbers which stand as symbols of life that seem bad luck to us because they bring us the *law* of pain, or correction. There is no number name, person or thing that we need to fear, but there is *the line of most resistance* and *the line of least resistance*. We may *choose* which one of these lines we will use.

Some numbers and names give us a line of most resistance. Others are easier to us. There are always two roads that lead to the town—one under, one over the hill. Some like to sit in the shade and rest, while others like to run. The road over the hill is hard for the one who dislikes to climb; and the one who likes to run chafes under the necessity of sitting in the shade. Nevertheless, there is nothing unlucky about it for either of them. Both roads take each one to his destination; and no one, save the owner of the name himself, says that he must climb or sit by the way. The road is open, and, if they desire, they can change places anywhere along the route.

The *inside* numbers, 1-3-5-7-9-11, are the vibrations

THE PSYCHOLOGY OF SUCCESS

of those who prefer the lower and level road to the town—who like to sit in the shade and rest. The *outside* numbers, 2-4-6-8-22, are the symbols of those who like the hill road and prefer to run. There is no bad luck. There is only vexation of spirit and effort for those who find themselves on the wrong road.

To sit with folded hands when all the soul is pulsing to be active! To let the throng go by on the road to success and never to get a chance to use it! *This is hell*—what we call " bad luck." However, it is not any greater " bad luck " to those who have it than is the constant rush and creative stuff to those who long for the quiet of contemplation and the silence of the shady path.

" Long ago I was weary of noises that fretted my soul with its din. Long ago I was weary of voices whose music my soul could not win." This is the truth about both of these equations; and, finding ourselves here, parked on the wrong side of the street because the next lesson our soul needs to learn is the one of struggling to get out, we are apt to put the blame on something outside, and not where it belongs—*upon ourselves*.

Concord! This is the plan of life. But discord is just as great an incentive to growth as any other experience. When this knowledge is ours we can place ourselves where everything is concordant, for we have learned how to elevate the higher vibrations and to subdue the lesser into a great symphony, how to live in conscious intensification of the qualities of mind we elect to use, and to make our number symbols carry us into them. Each year we must find ourselves a bit richer, happier, healthier, more successful, more contented, or there is something wrong with our system of *thinking, acting* and *speaking*. Maybe there is some-

WESTERN SYMBOLOGY

thing in our number vibrations which is a check upon our situations.

When we have thoroughly digested all of these causes we may deliberately change our name and bring to ourselves new vibrations and the things which they represent. Then we come to the question of what name we shall choose. Sometimes we do not like the names we have been given at birth, because as we grow and increase in understanding we feel the limitations of our old symbols. We cannot reach the ideals of our present incarnation with the lash of the past over our heads. " We must build more stately mansions for our soul as the swift seasons roll." Therefore, we either sink our names back into disuse or we boldly cancel them and select new ones. Not having the power or courage to do either, we drag on, discontented and unsuccessful.

When shall we change our names? What sort of a name shall we choose? These are the two questions all numerologists have to answer. A name should be changed whenever we dislike it, or whenever we have found that under it we are limited and unsuccessful. We should change our names when we have outgrown them. We have outgrown our names when we no longer care for the things which they attract. We should change our names when our given names are in opposition to each other—odd and even concords—or when they are in opposition to our surname, also, when our given names register the number symbols of 16, 14, 19.

Through our higher consciousness, and with conscious selection, we can build more stately mansions for our life work. We need not to have the ball and chain of old Karma dragging at our feet. We may choose new names which are more suited to our present needs.

Do we escape old Karma by simply changing our names? No! "Not one jot or tittle of the law will pass away," but our new names give us a new armour and they fit us more worthily to satisfy the old balance sheet of our past. We modify our experiences and protect ourselves in much the same way as we do when we put up a big, strong umbrella in a downpour of rain, or use a new windshield on our high-powered car.

Whenever failure dogs our efforts over a length of time we must look to our names, and we will soon find where we have been submerged.

One season I engaged a young man as a stenographer. He was out of work, and he had all the appearances of the depression and failure atmosphere. After watching his work for a few days I said, " Have you ever been lucky? You have had a hard life, haven't you?" He answered: "My life has been a regular hell. Life has certainly handed me a rotten deal."

The signs were written everywhere, because his first name worked out to 14, his second name to 16, and his last name to 2. As comrades in all his life he had the Great Destroyer, the Falling Tower, and the inefficiency of a negative 2. Reducing the 14 to 5, the 16 to 7 and adding 2, 5 plus 7 equals 12; this reduced to 3 and added to the 2 of his surname equals 5. As this 5 represents the love of change, self-indulgence, sex appetite and self, it was not hard to see that life as it stood could not give him great gifts.

His name was changed to vibrate with his heart's desires, which were to be associated with a big concern in a clerical way. In a month he answered an advertisement along the very line of his concentration, and he was accepted under his new name to vibrate him into 22-8. When I saw him two years later he was still with the firm, steadily going on towards his goal.

Life is too precious to let it drag on with hope dead within the breast. "God has provided some better things for us, which without us cannot be made perfect."

When life does not deliver, we must change our thoughts, or change our names, or readjust those that we have. We must move our desires with no uncertain hand, and push aside the rubbish which stands in our way.

LI. SITUATIONS, PLACES AND THINGS

EVERY situation, every place and every thing has a vibration. We learn their real character by number symbols, just as we do with people.

We begin to learn millinery, or we want to be a stenographer, or an electrician, et cetera, but we forget to study the symbols of the word. We know nothing of our harmonious or inharmonious adjustment with these things. If we want to be happy, we must be married to places, situations and things just as we are married to our affinity. Our soul numbers (the number of the vowels in our name) must be similar in situation, place and things if we are to find peace.

For example, we come to *Hotel Howard*. Taking its vowels we find that its soul number is:

$$11 \quad + \quad 7 \quad = 18 = 9$$
$$6 \; 5 \qquad 6 \; 1$$
$$\text{HOTEL HOWARD}$$

If our soul vibration is 11-7, or 11, or 7 alone, or 9 we will be happy at this hotel.

Or, we move to Asher Street, into house No. 1249. The soul number of Asher Street is:

$$6 \quad + \quad 10 \quad = 16 = 7$$
$$1 \; 5 \qquad 5 \; 5$$
$$\text{ASHER STREET}$$

The number of the house 1249 equals 16—7. We may find rest there if we can get through the two sixteens, or if our own soul number is 7 made up of 16;

WESTERN SYMBOLOGY

but it will be a hard task for any other number symbol, as its total is 7 plus 7 which equals 14.

We often wonder why situations, things and places affect us adversely, while others give us peace and happiness, never realising that we are under the law of opposites, similars or complementaries.

Whenever we want to be sure of our happiness we should find our own soul numbers, and compare them with the soul number of every place, situation or thing.

Suppose our name is Jane Jordan. The soul number is 13 or $(1+3)=4$.

The soul of Jane is 6, and the soul of Jordan is 7. Then 6 plus 7 is 13, and the digit of 13 is 4. Wherever we go we carry the soul of 4, and everything that has the soul of 4 is some more of the same thing, or some more of ourself. So any city, state, country, profession, work or speculation, place or thing, with a heart of 4 would be easy and peaceful to us. Other places would please or displease us according to whether they were opposites or complementaries. The soul of 3, 5, 7, 9 or 11 would be opposite to ours, while 2, 6, 8 or 22 would be complementary to us.

We could learn to live, work and rest with the soul of 2, 6, 8, or 22, but we would never be quite at peace with the opposite soul of 3, 5, 7, 9, or 11. We will only know real happiness with similars.

In choosing a profession, a career or business, we must always look to the quality of our soul number symbol and mate it with its own. The word "stenographers" has the soul of 8 and this is a power vibration, and demands skill and mentality. This is why there are so many inefficient stenographers. They do not have the soul of the work.

There are always some people who are much better

at their work than others are, no matter in what situation you find them. This is because they are more affinitized through their vibrations. It is difficult to work with what is entirely opposite to your own being.

The soul of millinery is 5.

Those who have 5 as their soul vibration are the ones who can tell at a glance what is becoming to themselves or to others. There are women with unlimited means whose hats are freakish because they are not artistic.

The word electrician is 11 in its soul.

The soul of an 11 is light, so electricity becomes just some more of himself if expressed through 2 and 9.

It is impossible to name all the different expressions of work, places or things, but the law holds good in everything.

What shall we eat? The answer is plain. Where is our soul vibration? Where shall I go? What city holds our soul number? We cannot quarrel with our own substance.

I am often asked: " I want to make a change. Where shall I go? What city would be best for me?" I can only answer: " Where is your soul? What city has a soul like your own? You cannot fail where the inside vibration and environment are in harmony.

LII. THE MYSTIC POWER OF GEMS, COLOURS, AND FLOWERS

WHAT are our gems? Just those which hold the *same* soul number. The soul of a *topaz* is 7, and belongs to all that number symbolizes. The soul of *pearl* is 6. And what jewel does a loving husband most long to give to his wife? The 6 is the vibration of home and domesticity. So when we hunt for the soul of things, places and situations our talisman is in our own vibrations.

There are many gems and colours whose composite number is our soul number, and we will find a degree of affinity with any of these, but the very essence of ourselves can only come through the soul of things. The soul of *ruby* is 3. The soul of *amethyst* is 6. The soul of *turquoise* is 8. The soul of *emerald* is 11.

COLOURS

It is the same with colours. Whatever colour holds our soul number will never be objectionable to our vision or sensibilities.

FLOWERS

Flowers come to us by the same law. Every flower soul that matches our own is some more of us and we of it.

LIII. HOW YOUR YEARS ARE NUMBERED

THE CYCLE OF THE BIRTHDAYS

OUR birthday is a never-ending adventure. With each new year there come to us new opportunities and new channels of experiences. This gives us a chance to extract more and more understanding from each new experience.

We have the opportunity to enter into life from another angle. It is a new opportunity to change our methods to fit the new vibrations. When we are born and breathe in the first vibrations, the way begins, and it never again touches life at quite the same place. The first year of life brings its own growth in its own way. Every other year does likewise, until our days and years are done. We must begin to count our experiences *from the first birthday,* and every year thereafter, from birthday to birthday again. This gives us our permanent, personal vibrations which must continually be set into the universal vibration. Sometimes we find that our personal vibrations coincide with the universal one of the year. Again we find they are opposite. But ever and always we are engaged in fitting our own birth vibrations into power with the day, month and year.

When one is born in the first months, and can begin his birth vibration with the beginning of the year it seems a bit easier for him to understand how to adjust himself. But when the birthday comes toward the last of December, and one has only a few days left of the old year, it is natural for him to want to pass his vibration on to the New Year and to claim its substance. This is not the original plan. We must stick to the vibrations of the day we are born. Even if we are forty years old and the birthday comes on the 24th of December, 1928, our personal vibration for the next year will be the sum of 6 (24) plus 3 (12) plus 2 (1928), which equals 11. This will be the vibration of our lesson, even though the year soon passes to 1929 and brings on its new vibration. We will be obliged to carry the initiation of 11 through all the vibrations of the next year, and find it coloured with the vibrations of 3. Basically, however, our initiation will be found in the things of 11, and our success can come only when we emphasize the ideal of our birthday.

It is easy to get this equation clear in our mind if we just remember that if we were born on that day we would face the first year of life under that symbol. Our lesson for the first year of life does not change because in a few days or months the year's vibrations change. It carries straight on until the next year. Then, and then only, do we come out into another influence strong enough to take any part in our unfoldment.

It is of supreme importance to get *right* on the vibration of the year. Birthdays are occultly the key to our success in business, love and opportunity. They tell us when to stand still and to act. In them we have an occult law operating, and it acts so strongly that it takes more than the ordinary consciousness of men to turn back the tide of affairs and mould it to their will.

There is only wasted effort to push and to toil when the vibrations of our year all signal us to rest and to take it easy. There is just as little gain in struggling and longing for home and marriage when it is not our marriage year. It is a dead loss to sit around and wait when our year means action, and all our success depends on our making things snappy. We must get the true vibrations of our new birthday, and then, throughout the whole year we must obey the subtle law which we have set for ourselves. We must never lose our own point of power. Whenever our own vibrations and the universal are made harmonious we find that everything in the new year comes to us in our own way. *We have only to command—life obeys.*

You will find in a preceding chapter the whole story of what your birthdays mean to you. In the chapter " How to Forecast for Any Year," study carefully the methods necessary for your success under the vibration of your own year.

LIV. HOW TO ADJUST YOURSELF TO ANY YEAR

IN HEALTH, HOME AND BUSINESS

The number of the year is the key to our actions for that year. This number added to our day and month gives us our directions for the ensuing year. It is our guide book of affairs.

For example, if our birthday is June 1st, we add the day 1 and the month 6, which equals 7. Then, for example, take the year 1926, the digit of which is 9. 7 plus 9 equals 16 reduced to a digit equals 7. This is the vibration for 1926 and will last until the birthday in 1927.

This tells us that anyone who has this vibration will find it is one of rearrangement. That old thing will pass away and new experiences replace them. It will hold something of harassment and inner unrest, as 7 is composed of 1 and 6, which is the number of the Great Malefic and the symbol of " The Falling Tower."

Altogether it will not make for a very easy year, and those whose numbers fall in this date will do well to look carefully to their love, friendship and home relations, for unrest and change can easily creep in. Also some new breaks in their financial situations, and loss of money, as well as name, place and power may challenge them. But, to those who live understandingly and poised in this vibration of 7, there will come rest, peace and time for meditation and self-development.

It is well to remember that there is no use to begin any new thing in a 7 year. It is the Sunday of life.

THE PSYCHOLOGY OF SUCCESS

Six days we labour and do all our work. And, on the seventh year, as well as on the seventh day, we should look to our application and set all things so that when we meet the vibrations of 7 we can have time to do the things we have long wanted to do. Thus we are able to come away from the stress of activity and constant creation.

The 7 is a wonderful vibration, but it always forewarns us to go slowly, keep strong, wind up the old, keep silent, and to let new adventures alone. We should never worry, fear, or drive on in anxiety. It is a positive truth that while we hold our mental mastery the world cannot crumble from beneath our feet.

We must reckon all the number vibrations in this same way. Whatever the number means, that is what the year will mean to us. We cannot have a year whose digit does not fall in one of the vibrations of 1-2-3-4-5-6-7-8-9, or their multiple, so if we turn to the chapter on the meaning of numbers we can easily determine our experiences for any year.

The year alone brings its own vibrations. The year 1926 reduced to a digit is 9. Thus, this year will need more brotherhood and the laying of plans for more human methods, a closer understanding, and larger humanitarian views. Then, adding this 9 vibration to our own, we can see that while this 9 will modify in our personal sum, it will still run through all our year, and we can find its effects everywhere.

Suppose our birthday is January 1st. Then adding the first day to the first month makes 2. Adding this to 9 we have 11, and if this is our vibration of our year it means that our success for this year will come by intensifying all the big, idealistic forces we have in us, and by following, as far as possible, along the lines of spiritual things. If we do not know this, and sink our time, effort and money along the line of material things and physical endeavour we will fail. Not because anything fails except us. We have failed to see our line of least resistance. The good things of 11 are waiting for us, but we miss them by going in the wrong direction.

This example will answer for any year. Find your own personal year vibration, and the vibration of the present year, and learn just what you have to do.

LV. YEAR BY YEAR

These vibrations apply to any year

THE YEAR DIGIT OF 1

When the year is 1 for us it means strong individualization—standing firm in our own ideals and purposes—daring to think, be and do along our own independent conceptions. Never give up. Never subordinate. Stand fast in belief in our own soul vision, and go straight on. Never turn to right or left. Listen to all the advice we can get, and then do just as our own soul dictates. Advice is always good for nothing, except as it helps us to come to our own opinion. As our opinion is often the outcome of much advice which we have been offered, so the vibration of 1 means that we must keep a listening ear, but drive straight ahead, aided alone by our soul's white light.

THE YEAR DIGIT OF 2

When the year is 2 for us we must strengthen our friendships and look for success to come to us through attraction, and not through too much effort. The 2 is not expected to work alone at any time. The power of 2 is in association. We need only to drive in a bit closer to the thought of doing big things *with* others—not alone.

We may look for new friends, new opportunities and new privileges to come to us. Living, thinking and working for the good of the bigger things, with harmonious relationships with people, situations, and things, will be the ladder by which we can climb to the top in our own personal accomplishments.

THE YEAR DIGIT OF 3

WHEN our day, month and year vibration comes to 3 we may know that we are in for a happy year, free from responsibility and warm with popularity and opportunity. The 3 is the joy ride of life. It is a mixture of the things of earth and the ideals of accomplishment. We need not hunt for responsibilities in a 3 year. We should follow our desires as far as we can do so constructively.

This is the vibration of hope and fruition. All that we have sown will appear. This is when we reap and garner up. We can watch the new things appear. It is a year of expectation, rejoicing and satisfaction. If we have lived anywhere close to the laws of truth we can " come rejoicing, bringing in the sheaves."

THE YEAR DIGIT OF 4

WHEN the total of our day, month and year is 4 we know this is the time to buckle down to direct action. We must put all our force and genius into whatever we are doing, or whatever we want to do. " Whatsoever our hand findeth to do," we must do this with all our might. This is the vibration which calls for endeavour, no loitering—no slothfulness. Only constant, unremitting activity will crown our year with success.

The keynote of 4 is work and organization—with direction and control—with deliberate concentration. Nothing can escape successful growth and power. The 4 is not the year for holidays, delays, or waiting. It is the year to dig deep and build your hopes on the rock of success. Then when the changes and lightness of 5 reach us, we can stand still and fear not, for we know we have set our ambitions too deep for external things to disturb them.

The 4 always pertains to our own self and the other self. So through carefully organizing people, situations and things we find that we can sometime later leave our work and visions in the hands of others, and they will work on while we sleep. But whenever our year is in 4 vibration it is the time to plant, so that in 5 and 7 we may harvest. The 4 is conservation of energy. It is the first step in building sublime and perfect things that will stand the test of time. Success will be certain with deep insight and finer arrangements.

THE YEAR DIGIT OF 5

THE 5 is the vibration of the day, month and year which means personal freedom. It is the year of change, travel, new opportunities, new hope, new friends, new loves, new endeavours. This is the creed of the 5 year. We let go of old bondages, old ideas, and all old and fixed points of attachment in things, situations and people. It is useless to resist or to stick to old points of attachment. It is the vibration of change; and change is the watchword of progression. " Perhaps someone, to thee all unknown, may into pleasant pathways lead your feet." In a 5 year we should turn our face to the new and welcome whatever comes, because it is our life's own law. The 5 is the real opportunity year, the longed for time when opportunity will again knock at our door. If we live in the light of true freedom we can pass on with it into new levels of conquest.

WESTERN SYMBOLOGY

THE YEAR DIGIT OF 6

THE year of 6 is the year of divine protection. It means a smaller orbit with safety. It is the growing towards the center of home, love, children, domesticity and responsibility. It means comfort, friendliness, and the joy of living with other people, things, and situations that we love. There is no need for hurry, but no langour; just calm and undisturbed, content. It is not a travelling year, but rather one that makes for activities in a smaller way.

The 6 is always a finishing year. We assort, tie up and store the things of our previous experiences, for we are on the way to 7, and a true 7 never carries much baggage. We must put everything where it belongs in a 6 year and leave it to work its own way to righteousness. It is not so much a year of effort as one of contented possession. There is in it loss and gain, for the old discards go hand in hand with the new selections. In a 6 year we can live in the realization of work well done, and enjoy the companionship of our true friends and the happiness of the things we have had the power to make our own.

It is not the vibrations of new beginnings as much as transmutation and finishing of what we have begun. With a 6 fully perfected we know that effort is no longer necessary, and "He also serves who only stands and waits." No really BIG things are ever done in a 6 year unless they are things which relate to home, love or religion. The BIG productions of life wait for the vibrations of unrest and great vision. But the 6 has what no other number has to such a full per cent.— protection, safety and contentment. It is the *marriage* vibration, and in it we can hope to come *face to face with our very own.*

THE YEAR DIGIT OF 7

The 7 vibration is the real fruition. It is the brooding time which comes before a fuller cycle. In a 7 year we ought to be able to sit quietly and in undisturbed peace reach our desires without effort. " Having done all, stand! " is the slogan of 7, and this means retreat and rest. Having done our best with all our might, we can rest in the law of our highest desires, and know that we are one with them. That assurance we cannot lose although " stars may fade and heaven fall," for our own is just what we have created for ourselves through all the other years of effort and endeavour.

The 7 year is the time to be alone. Although things seem to leave us, we know that we will find them again, retreating time is over. And they will be stronger and better. Life is from the Alone to the Alone. There must be a year when we are obliged to retire to *our own within*, and find there—in our own spirit—a wider view and a stronger power through the elimination of the old and a finer selection for the future years.

The 7 is the year to let business rest just as it is. It is not the year for changes, but for digging in deeply along the old lines, absorbing changes but resolving all things into finer methods and finer balances, waiting until 8 comes along and leads out into name, place, and power. It means stand still. Cultivate the interior. Wait! Have faith. Never give up. Self control. Self discipline. The 7 is the tomb of action, but from it comes the new success that had its roots in the silence and tranquility of the 7 substance.

WESTERN SYMBOLOGY

THE YEAR DIGIT OF 8

THE 8 is the year of renewed action. We must start again. Know all—do all—claim all—distribute all—and stand in a divine almightiness.

In the 8 year we must think, act, plan, and move with a master hand. Success comes only to us because we compel. It does not wait around through the months and then unexpectedly drop into our lap. And even if everything is ready for our good fortune, we can send it past us by a negative, spineless position. The 8 means power, publicity, approval, and positions of great eminence. And this holds true with every person, place, or thing. If one has a business, and jumps into it all over again in an 8 vibration it will improve along every line. If he has waited for a position he can make a new contract in an 8 year and win. The 8 is action—pep—grit—and a staying power which is not found in the other vibrations.

In 8 we may gather our forces to a high power pressure and mould life to our will. This is the year for enlargement along all lines of action. It calls for a larger vision and a stronger courage with more daring. " Faint heart never won fair lady " is true. Life has everything in it that we could possibly desire, and it is waiting to be acted upon. We are the actors; and nobody gives to us but ourselves. In an 8 year it is up to us to get right into the middle of this divine channel and demand our own.

This is the year of big things and big opportunities; we must be big enough to secure them. Our point of attraction and the thing which we want must be equal. This is the *power* vibration—the great opportunity. In this 8 vibration we can " kiss the lips of our desires."

THE PSYCHOLOGY OF SUCCESS

THE YEAR DIGIT OF 9

The 9 is the Great Challenge. The day, month, and year that vibrates to 9 means the full measure of ourself. We will meet everything that we can accomplish on all planes. It is not an easy year, because it will surely stage situations for us which will require strength and wisdom to meet. However, when it is past we will rejoice at the larger consciousness these tests have awakened. It is the balancing of forces. Whatever is in arrears must be brought up to a finish. Things that have dragged for a long time, situations that have been unsatisfactory, people who have blocked our progress —all these will assume a challenging position and, if possible, they will block our own progress. Through love and service, we must send ourselves on, past all difficulties.

The 9 is also a year of love, friendship, and happiness. We find that everything helps us and our desires accomplished,—if we dare to be strong, if we dare to hold fast to what we know to be true.

The 9 means "paid in full." When we have successfully passed the 9 year we are going on into 10, which means *individuality plus*, or the rest place of personal desires with the divine protection of the cipher. But the 9 will carry with it the vibrations of resistance until we learn to meet cheerfully everything which it brings. "Suffer it to be so now," is the slogan of the 9. Whenever we can say, "Go, Heaven!" we will find that Heaven turns right around and comes to us.

The 9 is the heart of life. As we pass through it, we have only to keep a pure heart, a clean mind, which is non-resisting but will understand our power. These things will be our armour of success, wherever we may find ourselves,—in business, at the home, or abroad.

WESTERN SYMBOLOGY

THE YEAR DIGIT OF 10

THE 10 year brings us a new beginning. We may use this opportunity to begin again all the things we have tried and have not accomplished. We can sort out, fix over, rearrange, discard and finish—then send out again under a new name and in a new fashion. We bring with us into 10 all that we have left from the 9 experiences, and therefore we are stronger and more confident in our endeavours.

The 10 is a great creative year. And this is our last days at school. For when we add the other one and make 11 we have so plussed ourself that we must have a big individuality to live up to it. The 10 is a *transition* number in which we may rise from all the dead things to the level of more privileges and more success. It is the open door of the mystical house, and through this door we pass from perfecting into being. The 10 always means a perfecting in something. The cipher of 10 shows that it is a resting place where we may select and use all that we have begun in other vibrations. When we add the last 1 we are out again into the sentient life of a higher cycle, in which much is given and much is required.

THE YEAR DIGIT OF 11

THE 11 is the year for inner development. We have finished the outer man in the 10, and now we must look to our growth on the inside. If it is *business* we must look to the very heart of our industry, and develop that rather than the extension channels.

The 11 means ideality, reverence and worship, and

THE PSYCHOLOGY OF SUCCESS

business will succeed in this year only if it is kept illumined with the highest methods of honesty, kindness and worthiness, all kept trimmed and burning. Our soul must be lit up with clean purposes—kept warm, genial and well filled with finer aspirations. Then we will succeed far beyond our most sanguine expectations. This is the vibration when the race is *not* to the swift or to the strong, but by the *Spirit*. If we keep close to that " Light which lighteth every man, coming into the world," we will be led by our intuition to make the right moves in every direction, and it will not be possible for us to be misguided by external influences.

The 11 is mother, home, love, heaven. By standing firm in all its vibrations we become heir to all these gifts of the Spirit.

THE YEAR DIGIT OF 12

The 12 is the year of perfected personal desires and purposes. This 12 reduces to 3, and, as 3 is the joy ride of life, this year takes on all of these things *plus*. Whatever we can say of 3 can be said doubly of 12. In this year we have a right to expect to gather where we have sown; and our harvest will be great if our seeding has been good. It all depends upon what we have put into the years.

The 12 is the year of finals. We must pass our examination in a big way. The best way to do that is to stand steadfast in our plans and purposes, and never wavering. For, in the 12 year, we can take out of life just what we have put in. When this year passes out and the new year comes in, whether it leaves us happy and joyfully contented or filled with regrets, unsatisfied longings, and deep resentment against life, will depend upon just how we have met the things we have given to ourselves.

We have nothing to do in 12 but to balance our books and to get ready for a new plunge into life when the books of the new year open. We must set our debit and credit and go on,—either mortgaged to life or free and untrammeled.

LVI. THE MONTHS

January ....Active, creative life
February ....Repose—friendships
March ....Joyful activity
April ....Concentrated energy
May ....Life more abundant ✸
June ....Conscious creation
July ....Silence and meditation—waiting
August ....Reinforced creativity
September ....Submerged in humanity
October ....Re-emerged in creative self-hood
November ....Spiritual vision intensified
December ....Self satisfaction—completion

LVII. SUMMARY OF MONTHS AND YEARS

These are the qualities of months and years. We can link them with our own individual vibrations and bring to ourselves the best things which life has to give, for " knowledge is power."

> To know—to see—to understand—
>   To watch life's changes come and go—
> What matter if we touch the burning sand,
>   If through it all we find Life's After-glow!

All other vibrations which follow after 12 are simply duplicates of the single numbers, and can be reckoned with from these. They are all the single numbers, only *plus* in their vibration. This quality of their plus is determined by the number preceding. For example:

If the number is 13 the vibration is 4. If it is 24 the vibration is 6. If it is 36 the vibration is 9, and so on.

The months of the year can be reckoned by the same standards of vibrations. For business success, it is well to divide the months into Physical, Mental, Emotional and Spiritual numbers, and to act accordingly.

EXAMPLE

January	Mental—physical
February	Physical—emotional
March	Emotional—mental
April	Mental
May	Physical

June ....Emotional—mental
July ....Mental—spiritual
August ....Mental—emotional
September ....Emotional—mental
October ....Mental—emotional
November ....Spiritual—physical
December ....Emotional—mental

There is no profit in doing business in a physical or emotional way when it is a mental month; and there is no chance that we can have our greatest success when we do business in an intuitional way in a mental month. *Physical* means attention to form and basic principles. *Mental* means close attention to details and finer organization. *Emotional* means close attention to people and their wants—strengthening the good will of business. *Spiritual* means attention to the larger extensions of business and building a larger vision of opportunity and success.

In taking heed of these business pointers we can make a success along these higher laws of understanding. We can stay successful, for we do not attain success by mysterious, unknown ways, but through conscious use of life's finer forces.

LVIII. PERSONAL ACTION IN THE YEAR

A SUMMARY

1

IF our vibration is 1 we should be active, stirring, and begin new things. Think our own thoughts. Be the divine thinker of our own thoughts, and be up and doing with a heart for any fate.

2

The advice to a 2 is to wait. Don't push. Be quiet and collected. Suffer things to be as they are. Effort is not necessary! "He also serves who only stands and waits."

3

A 3 should express itself along some agreeable line. <u>Do something he has put off doing</u>. Look out for new avenues of personal activity. Be more agreeable than ever, and never pick up a thought of worry about tomorrow.

4

If our vibration is 4 we should <u>get down to it and work</u>. Do everything that has been <u>neglected</u>. "<u>Procrastination is the thief of time</u>." Don't lag behind or shirk. Push everything ahead, and never rest until all our desires are accomplished—until our <u>good is better</u> than our <u>best</u>.

5

A 5 should change his plans, and expect things to change for him. There will be new opportunities, new friends. It is the time to travel, to seek new experiences, and to expand all lines of business and endeavour.

6

If our vibration is 6, this is a home year—a marrying year. It is the time to intensify home ideals, but is not the time to make changes. Stick to the usual things; it is not the vibrations for big ventures. Finish all the things you have begun.

7

This is the Sunday of life. Try not to strive. Rest! Neither attempt to finish the old nor to begin the new. Be content—poised. This is a growing time. Don't try to crush the buds of life to blooming. Do your best, think your desires—and wait.

8

This is a power year. It is good for action—new business—extension of business—change of interests—new impulses—new directions of power.

9

This is the friendship year. Expect much from friends. Give much. Cherish duty and opportunity. It is a good year for pleasure, for pleasing things and people; and for the silencing of strife. Love—truth—peace is its keynote. More power through conquests.

11

This is the year for Spiritual growth. There should be devotion to holy things this year, non-resistance, silence, and usefulness along religious lines.

22

This is our power year. Plunge into your desires. Make big plans. Never take " No " for an answer. In association and in leadership is your power. Set the pace for all you desire, and make the situation for all of it to work out. You need not go slow. Do your best.

LIX. HOW TO SET ANY COMING EVENT

CONVENTIONS, INTERVIEWS, MEETINGS, PUBLICITY, ET CETERA.

THERE are many times when we would like to be able to determine just what sort of vibrations we may meet in some coming event, like the opening of a new play, a new business, or moving into a new situation. And, sometimes, we would like to follow events from days to months and on to the happenings of the year.

In order to do this we must first take the vibrations of the day, for example, the 2nd or 3rd day. No matter what day it is, we just use the vibration of that number as our first symbol (*reducing all double numbers to the digit, remember!*). Suppose it is the 6th day of the month. Then this day will represent all the things which 6 stands for, and we may expect to find them intruding themselves into our day of happenings. Six always brings ideality, but it also brings responsibility, respectability and domesticity—home things—little things. And it has more power through people than through things.

In order to find the vibration of the month, do exactly the same thing. Find out just what month it is—the 1st, 3rd, 4th—any one. Suppose it is the 7th month—July. Then we know that July is bound to bring us the basic vibrations of 7, and whatever is contained in a 7 vibration we may expect to meet in this month.

If we want to find out what the day and month vibration will naturally condense into for us, we must add the number of the day and the month. Suppose it is the 3rd day of the 7th month. The 3 plus 7 equals 10. This will be the dominating vibration of the day for us. If you will read what 10 vibrates us into union with, there will be no confusion about just what this day will be like—if we live it in harmony with the positive things.

To get the vibration of the year we add all the numbers of the year together—1933 equals 16—1 and 6 equals 7. Thus we find the vibration of the year is 7. We gather from this that 1933 will be a very introvert year, and humanity will turn naturally to a study of the things of the inner life. Adding our own day and month vibration to the vibration of the year will always tell us just what the year will mean for us. Supposing that our day was the 2nd of March—the 3rd month. These reduced, equal 5. Added to 7 of the year 1933 we have 12—digit 3. All yearly vibrations are found this way. If this is our vibration we may be sure that if we live up to all the positive vibrations of 3 we will have a year of happiness, prosperity and change, with the joy ride of life—great success and harmony.

EXAMPLE

A convention is to be held on May 2nd. Here we have the 2nd day and the 5th month, which equals 7. This vibration is a stationary vibration, and all conventions ever held on this day and month will come in under the same law of happenings—only the difference in the vibration of the year will make the difference in all other conventions. Thus 1929 will lend 3 to the final, which will make the whole day, month and year 10, with its own actions of people, situations and things. Again

WESTERN SYMBOLOGY

1932 will lend 6 to the day and month, 7, which will make 13, or 4. This convention of 1932 will be a very different expression from the one of 1929.

When we know these number symbols we can always be sure of just what we are heading into, no matter what it may concern, and we can so adjust ourselves to the eventual vibrations that we never need to say we were disappointed or failed to get what we expected. If we do we can know it is our own fault.

PERSONAL RELATIONS TO EVENTS

When we have established the vibration of the day, month and year of the convention we often want to know just what we will get out of it for ourselves. In order to know this we must take our own birthday date —day, month and year—and find whether our vibration is in the law of similars, opposites, or complementaries, with the vibration of the convention.

The law of concords runs through every action of life. In the vibration of opposites we can no more hope to find perfect happiness at a convention, an opening, or organization of a new company, a new beginning of anything, or a closing of the old, than we can hope for a happy union with one who is not in sympathy with our own selfhood.

EXAMPLE

Suppose the sum total of the day, month and year of the convention, or of the new thing, summed up to 6. Our vibrations summed up to 5. Reading the meaning of these two vibrations is enough to teach us that we would likely have a very dull time at the gathering, and that very little would be done there in accordance with our ideas or methods. When we go blindly and are disappointed we know why. These vibrations can give us a very clear clue to every future event. Where we have authority, it is wise to select the vibrations for any important thing which will be bound to make it a success, and which will harmonize with our own actions and desires.

Every event carries with it a very pronounced personal vibration of its own, and when our own vibrations are opposite we suffer. When our vibrations coincide we are happy and full of hope of accomplishment. Similarity always gives a definite colour to every event.

LX. HOW TO ATTRACT MONEY

In dealing with money we must fulfil every law of money. We must have banking days in material vibrations. We must keep a material amount on deposit. We must never neglect the depositing hour, or carry money about carelessly, crumpled and loose in pockets or bags. Money has the soul of 11; and its material body and mind are 16 = 7. So money has wings, and it flies away whenever the law of its delicate soul is transgressed.

Did you ever see a poor man with fine, smoothly folded bills? Did you ever see a rich man with crumpled, soiled ones? Life tells its own story and has its own signs. All money is God's money, or spiritual substance. The mystics say that at its soul it carries the mystical vibration.

To attain success in banking we must choose the number symbols of our names that relate with the physical or the mental plane, 1-2-4-7-8-22, and bank for any great purpose on any one or on all of these days. The 3 is a weak banking vibration, as 3 is a scattering number and does not make for accumulation. The 3 lives to the full measure of its desires.

The 5 is also a reckless deposit day, as it is full of chance and change—up to-day and down to-morrow—and money travels fast in this vibration. The 5 lives *to live*. It is the gambling vibration on which we have to take a chance.

The 7 is the number to use in a savings bank deposit, but not in the usual moving deposit. The 7 holds—

THE PSYCHOLOGY OF SUCCESS

closes in—does not distribute, but is safe, trusty and sure to remain. Used as a regular checking deposit vibration it is limited and <u>not given to increase</u>.

It is just as easy to work *with* the law of money as *against* it, once we know it. It is also necessary that we keep some money somewhere on deposit, in order to fulfil the cosmic law of accumulation. It is pure <u>foolhardiness</u> to <u>check the last $1</u> out of the bank. It is written: "Give me a fulcrum and I will move the world." The reason why some people are always bankrupt is because they have destroyed their fulcrum.

It is a mystical law that "To him that hath shall be given, and to him that hath not, even that which he hath shall be taken away." This is true in regard to money as well as in regard to other things. We always need to have a money fulcrum, with which the law of money can move our material universe into form. The *soul* of money *in* the bank is one *with* the money of the *world*—1-2-4-8-22. This allows a wide margin for depositing, and closes the fatal doors through which money slips away.

1
2
4 - 22
8

LXI. BUSINESS SIGNATURES

WHY FAMOUS MEN AND WOMEN CHANGE THEIR NAMES

When we drop some of our names and condense a signature we do not lose the vibrations we are using, pouring all of our activity through the few channels instead of the many. It is one of the ways of concentrating force. John Henry Harrison slips all of himself into J. H. Harrison or J. Henry Harrison. He emphasizes 1-8 with all the vibrations of Harrison, 8-1-9-9-9-1-6-5, which means power, individuality, generality, respectability, and freedom.

It is a well-known fact that <u>business signatures are always shortened</u>. Business signatures should be chosen according to what one desires. *Real Estate* success comes in under 2-4-6. *Dramatic* success under 1-9-11. *Leadership and Management* under 4-8-22. All business signatures should mate the soul's desire. One will never get rich in business with the signature of a dramatist, nor prosper in music or drama with the signature of a blacksmith.

We must sign the number symbols of our names which accord with our desires. This is why actors, movie stars, and writers of the present day <u>change their names to fit their vocations</u>, and find success where before they found failure.

LXII. POSITIVE AND NEGATIVE NUMBERS

THEIR QUALITIES OF CONSCIOUSNESS

POSITIVE 1

LEADERSHIP, originality, special work, able to work alone, pioneer, strong, dominant, forceful, daring, creative, brilliant judgment, courageous, independent, separatist, fearless, nonconformist, popular for their power and ability.

NEGATIVE 1

Stubborn, hard, fault finding, conceited, resentful, narrow-minded, obstinate, immovable, agitator, socialist, anarchist, rule or ruin, separate, uncontrollable, self-willed, biased, judgment is weak and vacillating, no ego development. Absence of all positive character of 1.

POSITIVE 2

The great mixer, diplomatist, association, counsellor, gentle, non-resistant, easy going, fond of simple pleasures, settlers, investors, not ambitious, buffers and middlemen, never alone, fond of friends and much company, make good and faithful friends.

NEGATIVE 2

Idle, non-existant, self-depreciative, morose, sullen, weak, easily influenced, lazy, careless, full of sloth, often a falsifier, quitter, irresponsible and lacking interest, unreliable in friendship and business, no ultimate aim, drifters, often friendless and bitter, left behind by the normal type.

POSITIVE 3

Entertaining, fine disposition, happy, inspiring, never troubled, self confident, independent, irrepressible, faithful in friendship, good imitators, changeable in likes and dislikes, polite, efficient, attractive, generally popular.

NEGATIVE 3

Changeable, untrustworthy, conceited and self-righteous, spiritual pride, sullen, unexpressed, tiresome, complaining, petulant, idle, no friends, disliked for self conceit, exaggerated likes and dislikes, unpopular.

POSITIVE 4

Self-reliant, kind, exact, brusque, hard, good worker, plodder, deliberate, unemotional, just, not too generous, balanced and conventional, trustworthy, self-sacrificing, make good judges, great responsibility is a pleasure, are corner stones of society and service, not too popular but respected.

NEGATIVE 4

The driver, miser, critic of people, law giver, inexorable, intolerant, unmerciful, self-opinionated, egotistical, unrelenting, resistful and hard to please, obeyed but not loved.

POSITIVE 5

Jolly, easy, irrepressible, excitable, fond of change, active, forceful, influential, not too reliable in all things, good liver, pal, and friend, dislikes convention, follower of new orders and ideas, good traveller, popular everywhere, fearless, good gamblers on all chances, obliging, frank and popular.

NEGATIVE 5

Lawless in sex appetite and selfishness, irresponsible, faithless, cowardly, spendthrift, profligate, borrower, untrustworthy, bluffer, untruthful, waster, lose their friends through excesses, often unpopular and discarded.

POSITIVE 6

Loving, kind, forgiving, full of comfort, steady, enduring, unchangeable, generous, patient, non-resistant, helpful, full of cheerfulness, give more than they get, no malice, can wait, giver of good words, honest, irreproachable, always popular, friend of children, lover of home.

NEGATIVE 6

A drudge, full of self-sympathy, discontented, jealous of others, suspicious, restless, complaining, lonely, separate, unsympathetic, coveteous, comparing, troublesome to everybody, worried about friends, and always pitied by them.

POSITIVE 7

Uncompromising, silent, introspective, unexpressed, tolerant, long suffering, loves deeply and permanently, kind, sympathetic, untiring, dislikes people and crowds, love of nature and aloofness, comforts others, keeps secrets, unwearying allegiance to business and duty, conventional and proper, not popular at first, but wins later, silence and meditation is their strength.

NEGATIVE 7

Morose, gloomy, sarcastic, a babbler, when they should be silent, unapproachable, fault-finding, miserly, critical, never smiling or happy, self-analytical, morbid, unpopular and left to die alone.

POSITIVE 8

Strong, self-reliant, helps himself and others, pride is in efficiency, controller, director, leader, starter and finisher, forges way anywhere, popular, much to be depended upon by others, just, judge and law giver, kind, generous and loyal, always has money, backbone of the world, and his popularity makes him the guest of the world.

NEGATIVE 8

Tyrannical, insular, abusive, egotistical, superior, revengeful, feared but never loved, often hated, scheming for own good, sweat-shop boss, bloated aristocrat of wealth and power, bully of the world, unpopular but often powerful.

POSITITVE 9

Loving, humanitarian, philanthropic, entertaining, charitable, genial, forgiving, busy with welfare work for the world, giving of time, money and self, merciful, truthful, beloved of all the world, hated by none, approved and popular, comforter of the world.

NEGATIVE 9

Faithless, profligate, breaking hearts, untruthful, over charitable, self-indulgent, free lover, irregular in business, seeking approval, working for flattery, popular but unreliable, loving self more than service.

LXIII. HOW TO WRITE A SYMBOLSCOPE

Whether we read verbally or write out the number symbols and their vibrations, we must set them in form so that they can easily be interpreted.

First: Write *all* the given names and the surname. Then draw a straight line close above the top of the name and another below the name.

On the top line we place the number value of the vowels, reducing them to digits. Then, drawing another line, we add all the vowels of the given names. Reduce these to a *digit* and add them to the digit of the surname. The surname, like the year, is permanent; so all other vibrations, no matter how many, must be reduced and absorbed into the permanent vibrations of the surname. They must be reduced to a digit before they are added to the digit of the surname. *Remember this.*

The *total* of this is again reduced and placed at the right hand end of the line. This number symbolizes the Soul Vibration, the heart, the individuality, the reality of the magnet called *man*. This is the " I am " expressed in all.

Second: Place the number of *consonants* below the lower line. Reduce as above. Add the number of consonants and place the final digit at the right-hand side of the lower line. This is the Personality vibration, or the symbol of what is behind the name—the story of his past experiences and the key to his appearance.

Third: Place the value of each letter in the name, vowels and consonants, below the lower line, then add as before. Reduce and place the total at the right-hand side of the last line. This is the Destiny—the Composite Self—the Vocation Number—the riddle of the future, what is bound to happen. It is the quality of consciousness the individual will take with him when he dies. It is the sum total of his accumulative consciousness.

Fourth: Write the day of the month, the number of the month, and the year of birth. Add the digits of the day and month, then reduce to a digit and add it to the digit of the year. This is the number-symbol of the *Grade* in the School of Life. The evolving ego has to take all of the initiations many times. He must pass from 1 to 9 in common experiences, then pass as a teacher, leader, elder brother, master messenger. The vibrations of the day is his initiation up to 25 years of age. The vibrations of the month marks the experience up to 50 years of age. The year vibrations show his final and closing experiences.

The initiation symbols show the different periods of growth. The number vibrations up to 25 years of age show the experiences of that period. The number vibrations of the month mark the middle period. The number vibrations of the year mark the finals of life.

The single numbers in initiation show the normal experiences. The higher numbers in initiation, 8 and 9, show leadership and mastery, and the double numbers 11-22-33-44-55-66-77-88-99, etc., show messenger and masters.

When in adding the number symbols we come to a name that numbers 11-22-33-44-55, or any of the double vibrations, we do not need to add these to the single numbers. We can let these stand on their own value. We simply show the *quality* of the *Initiation*. When the symbolscope is all set up, it is easy to interpret, by following the principles presented in this book. We

WESTERN SYMBOLOGY

need only intelligently to connect things in their finer relationships and can read the symbolscope by the number-symbols we find registered.

We can secure much or little out of the number symbols, according to the degree of our own understanding. The table is set by the *scope* itself, and whoever runs may read—if he knows how. And, to know *how*, beyond the slightest possibility of being mistaken, is the work of the *modern numerologist*. Here is an example:

JOHN HIRAM BAILEY

Born

	Day	Month	Year	
	21	9	1862	
Soul	6	1	6	= 13 = 4
	6	10	15	
	6	9 1	1 9 5	

JOHN HIRAM BAILEY

Personality	1 8 5	8 9 4 2	3 7	
	14	21	12	
	5	3	3	= 11
Destinw and	1 6 8 5	8 99 1 4	2 1 9 3 5 7	
Vocation	20	31	27	
	2	4	9	= 15 = 6

INITIATION

Day	Month	Year	Initiation
21	9	1862	
3	plus 9	17	
	12	8	
	3 plus	8 =	11

THE PSYCHOLOGY OF SUCCESS

We find in this *numberscope* that John Hiram Bailey has a soul of 4. That back of him, for his personality he also has 11. That he has a destiny of 15 = 6 and an initiation of 11.

By the time we subject John's vibration to the whole analysis of numerology, we will find that there is very little left that we do not know about him.

LXIV. HOW TO INTERPRET A SYMBOLSCOPE

When the symbolscope is set up correctly it becomes a subtle task to interpret what the symbols reveal. Much or little can be made out of it, according to the skill used in relating facts, causes and finer relationships.

No one who has not made himself familiar with all that symbology contains, can read a symbolscope and give a delineation that is worth while. Every number is *more than a number;* and every name is a passport into some secret chamber of human life.

When reading for anyone we should be able to tell him everything that his numbers reveal. Each one wants to hear all about himself, and he also wants to know why, where, how and when. Just a few glittering generalities are not enough to make any science valuable to anyone.

Everyone wants to be saved from the struggle of existence. He has a right to demand that he be linked up with the best that the world can give, and that he be given a fair chance to make an intelligent effort to attain his desires, with a free hand to clean up any state of mind that is limiting his advancement.

Everyone in the world does the very best he knows how. When he knows better he will do better. All that anyone asks is that some one else who does *know how* shall fix his own *know how*. When this is done he will rescue himself, for once we *know* we can never *not know*.

When we read a symbolscope we must dissect the seeker from every angle. Sometimes it takes almost a spiritual sleuth to seek out the subtle lines of relationship which make for failure or success. It requires very great caution in the selection of number-symbols when ever we attempt to change a name. We should closely watch the soul and the desire—also the vocational vibration—for it is always imperative that we should be able to do the things we long to do. Our point of attraction and the thing which we want must be equal.

If we follow this table in reading a symbolscope we will soon become familiar with it. We can easily pick up a name anywhere and subject it to a severe grilling for faults and power.

When reading it is not necessary to tell all the faults and the negative vibrations we find. The world-mind is too infantile to stand for the naked truth about itself. But it is necessary for *us* to *know* it. It is our key to what is, has been and will be. However, when we interpret to the listener we need to tell only the things which are necessary for an antidote to the limiting things. We should explain from the angle of the biggest and best. When men learn to live up to the big things in them they may ignore the little traits.

A TABLE FOR THE INTERPRETATION OF A SYMBOLSCOPE

1. What is at the back of him
2. What is in him
3. What is ahead of him
4. His initiation
5. Inside and outside vibrations
6. Planes of expression
7. Cosmic vibrations
8. Entering and leaving numbers
9. Ciphers and their meaning
10. Power numbers
11. Novitiate, Initiate, Illuminati
12. Whom to marry
13. Wedding days
14. Naming children
15. Choice of life work
16. Vocations
17. Qualities of consciousness
18. Where to live
19. Business combinations
20. What vibrations are lacking

WESTERN SYMBOLOGY

21. Strong and weak points in character
22. Ruling Passions
23. Explain malefics in name and numbers
24. Give business advice
25. Read the years—past, present, and prospective
26. Tell how to change name, if necessary
27. Construct a power name according to his numbers
28. Give number of success and spiritual vibrations
29. Give methods by which he can increase spiritual growth
30. Sum up the whole character with final suggestions.

To take a name with *dates* and subject it to the fine occult inquiry that these things give, we will find that there is very little left which is not interpreted. When anyone really knows himself he can work with conscious harmony and rhythm toward health, wealth and happiness because the reward of perfect self-realization is always peace, power and plenty.

BOOK FOUR
The Soul's Refrain

BOOK FOUR

LXV. A SOUL'S REFRAIN

YOUR KEYNOTES, HUMAN CHORD, AND LIFE SONG

THE KEYNOTES

Whatever chord or key fits your soul vibration will never jar our sensibilities. The vibration of the:

Key of C is 1   Key of G is 5
Key of D is 2   Key of A is 6
Key of E is 3   Key of B is 7
Key of F is 4   Key of High C is 8
Key of High D is 9

THE HUMAN CHORD

The Cosmic Vibrations of Your Name

The human chord is simply the arrangement of all the number symbols in their relationship to the musical scale. C D E F G—A B C D E F G.

1 2 3 4 5 6 7 8 9
C D E F G A B C D

COLOURS

1. C is Red
2. D is Pink
3. E is Green
4. F is Violet
5. G is Yellow
6. A is White (Opaque)
7. B is White (Transparent)

From here we return to C and repeat over again.

WESTERN SYMBOLOGY

Sometimes the Human Chord is very harmonious, but few in this race consciousness have evolved far enough—body, mind, soul and spirit—to make a song of beauty and harmony. Sometimes it is almost a funeral dirge, because the evolution has come up so irregularly. Life hates a transgressor, and we must work carefully with the development of all our vibrations before we can produce the fourfold man and a perfectly harmonious human chord.

EXAMPLE OF HUMAN CHORD

```
JANE    JORDAN
1 1 5 5  1 6 9 4 1 5
C C G G  C A D F C G
```

LIFE-SONG

If we work out her "life-song" we do it by taking the number vibrations of her name; the final digits in these vibrations are her harmonies, or inharmonies.

```
                6  plus   7   equals 13 or 4 (Soul)
    1   5   6    1
  J A N E   J O R D A N
    1   5    1 9 4   5
       6  plus  19   equals 25 or 7 (Personality)
  1 1 5 5   1 6 9 4 1 5
    12   plus   26
    3    plus   8    equals 11 (Destiny)
        Key of F is  4 = Soul
        Key of B is  7 = Personality
        Key of D is 11 = Destiny
```

This will make a great discord, and it is true that in her ultimates, Jane Jordan has the law of opposites, 4

A SOUL'S REFRAIN

and 7. These indicate a conflict between the inner and the outer life. The 4 and 7 are mental numbers, while 11 is spiritual, so the conflict of opposites goes on.

When the life-song of Jane Jordan is played it should be composed of vibrations recombined for harmony.

" My heart is fixed,
Oh God, my heart is fixed."

This would do for Jane's life song.

These notes of Jane's numbers may be set on the musical staff. When played they bring out the harmony or discord of Jane Jordan's human chord. The inharmony of our inner discord sometimes can quite deaden our own inner ears, and our own souls go dumb with despair. And again, the divine harmony within is a glorious song, to which we can listen even while we labour in life's vineyard.

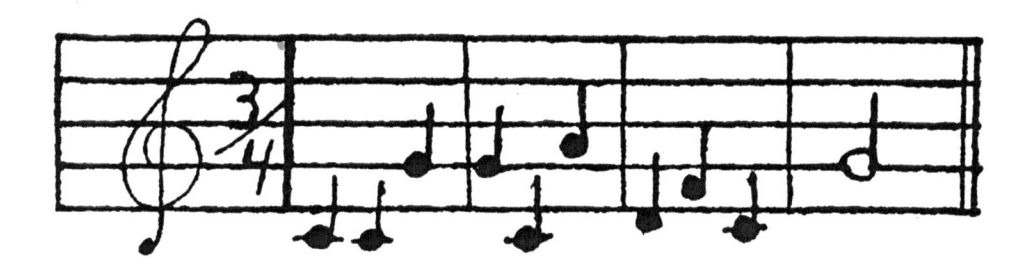

WESTERN SYMBOLOGY

LXVI. THE LAST WORD

THE whole ultimate of life is to know the SELF. Whenever we can really feel that we are no longer self-deluded we are nearing the edge of the path of wisdom.

When we can lay all our cards of life face up before us and read what is written there for us and for others, we gain some idea of the strength or weakness of the hand which we are playing.

There are rules for the Game of Life just as certain as the rules men have made for their game of cards. The back-wash of humanity is made up of those who have not, or will not, or cannot learn the rules of the game.

We must win our game of life with our own deck, and we cannot cheat, or expect others to help us at the risk of losing their own game. Our number-symbols are our deck of cards. There are power-symbols, and it is a waste of time and energy to play for success or for the attainment of our heart's desires with our number-symbols unknown and all the trump cards left in the deck.

When we find the whole of the *self* and know just what we have to plunge on we are safe in any man's land. We can stake our whole life on our game; for our understanding loads the dice which win.

When we know what is in our heart and soul we can rest our faith in that thing within us on which we can win. When we know what is ahead of us we can go fearlessly to meet it. When we know what is back of us we can rest on a reserve force which will be like reinforcements to a tired army.

A SOUL'S REFRAIN

Self-knowledge is the password into the great secret order of Life. We meet all the tests with courage and daring; for at the last initiation we find it was all a divine adventure.

We find that it strengthens us to know just how we really appear to others. We can strengthen the points of personality until we are one hundred per cent. pleasing, attractive and charming.

When we know whom to marry we will not go out on a senseless search for sensation and experience. We find a satisfying degree of harmony in living with everybody, and best of all, everybody can live with us and respect us. Numbers bear down on the law that sets everyone free, and shows that love must bring love. Power must rule. Freedom must be free. Noise will seek noise, and silence will remain silence, no matter where we find it.

Through business psychology we can place ourselves right in the middle of the swift channel of supply, and *win*,—not through others, but *with* others through the capacity we find in ourselves.

Health—wealth—love—prosperity—happiness — freedom—service—and worship is our eternal creed and they form our song of success. With these things locked fast in our heart we can speak with a voice of power wherever we go.

The first commandment of man to man was "*Know thyself*," and the fruits of this knowing are self-realization, self-control, self-expression, self-confidence, self-direction, and conscious evolution. We have then taken our evolution into our own hands and we can *claim* all, *possess* all and *distribute* all in a new Almightiness.

Nations may come and go, the seas retire and destruction lay earth's mighty cities low,—but symbology will always remain an eternal bridge between the things that have been and those which are yet to be. Men will turn to it again and again in glad surprise. With it they will re-translate their ever present into a perfect future which is revealed to them through the symbols of themselves.

INDEX

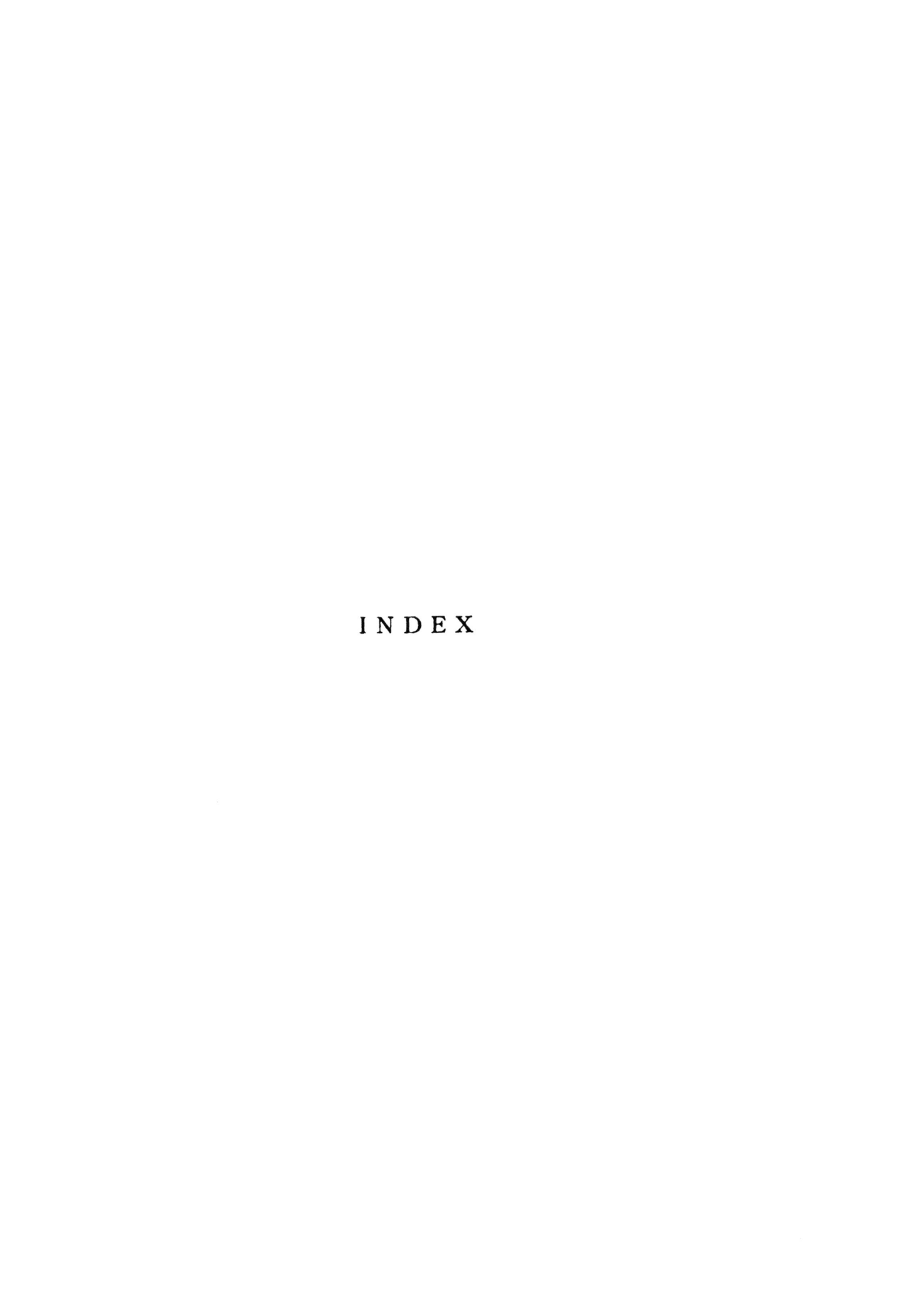

INDEX

Adjustment of self to number vibrations of the year 242
Accomplishment, and names, The Relation of...... 64
All, The, (The Illuminati) 43, 49, 123
Banking, Numbers and 262
Birth date, The meaning of................................ 62
Birthdays, The Cycle of the.............................. 237
Brothers, The Two 74
Business misfits 199
Business, Number combination in 198
Business, Psychology of.................................. 191
Change of name does not do, What a.................. 230
Change of name, Illustration of a...................... 234
Change name, How and when to........................ 225
Change of name when consciousness has changed... 28
Character revealed by vowels, The...................... 55
Children, How to name 120
Choosing a profession or business...................... 238
Cipher vbrations, The.................................... 126
Colours and the human chord............................ 281
Colours 236
Cosmic vibrations 37
Complementary marriages 105
Complementaries 93
Combination of numbers in business.................... 198
Combination of numbers in marriage.................. 95
Coming events, How to set.............................. 258
Composite self, The...................................... 59

INDEX

Composite vibrations (22)	195
Concords, Odd and even	91
Consciousness, The four divisions of	190
Consciousness revealed by numbers, Our grade of	45, 51
Consciousness, The relation of names to	27, 86
Consonants as symbols of personality	170
Constructive numbers	209
Conventions, interviews, publicity, How to plan for	258
Cosmic law and initiations	62
Cosmic law and names	228
Cosmic vibrations	37
Covenant between parents and children, The	120
Cycles	79, 86
Cycles, How to find our personal	82
Cyclic vibrations, relation of personal to universal	86
Desires as revealed by names	55
Destiny	52
Destiny and destiny numbers	59
Destiny numbers and the choice of vocations	61
Destiny example, A	60
Digits of numbers, Their meaning in initiation	66
Digits of numbers, Their meaning in marriage	95
Digits of numbers, Their meaning in vocation	60
Doors, The Two	124
Double numbers	66, 80
Double numbers, The special meaning of	81
Eight, 9, 11, 22, 33, etc., The Third Degree (The All)	48
Eight as a power number	211
Eleven as a power number	213
Elemental forces	216
Emotional vibrations, 3, 6, and 9	192
Even and odd numbers	70, 232

INDEX

Events, How to set coming	258
Events, Personal relation to	260
Evidences of Symbology's trueness	15
Expression, The planes of	189
Extrovert, The	70
Fate	86
Fate number, The	62
Fate and number vibrations	64
Famous change their names, Why the	264
Five as a power number	210
Final, or ultimate, letters of names	124
First Degree, The, (1, 2, and 3)	45
First and last letters of names	124
Flowers	236
Four, 5, 6, and 7, The Second Degree, The	47
Four square in business, The	198
Fourteen	218
Gems	236
"Good" and "bad" numbers	229
Great Parade, The	44
Great Within and the great Without, The	70
Human Chord, Example of	282
Influence of vibrations on conduct	122
Inharmony, Types of	100
Illuminati Consciousness, The	49
"I never had a fair chance"	120
Initial letters of names	124
Initiate consciousness, The, (The Many) (4, 5, 6, 7)	47
Initiation	52, 62
Initiation and soul numbers, Importance of	120
Initiation and soul numbers, Their relation to personality in marriage	95, 119
Initiation example, An	64, 69
Initiation vibrations classified	66

INDEX

Initiation numbers and cycles	82
Intelligence, The planes of	23
Inner vibrations	72
Inside, or uneven, numbers	72, 232
Intensified numbers, (3, 7, and 9)	128
Introvert, The	70, 72
Introvert, The, An example of	76
Justice, (a poem), by Julia Seton, M.D.	185
Knowing self	277
Keynotes, The	281
Last Word, The (Knowing self)	277
Life-song	282
Life Vibrations, The four	52
Letters and numbers, The Origin of	27
Letters and numbers, Table of	28
Love marriage and divorce	91
Luck	215
"Lucky," or constructive numbers	209
Many, The, (4, 5, 6, 7)	43, 48
Malefic symbols, or numbers, Fourteen	218
Many letters in a name, The effect of	28
Malefic symbols, or numbers, Nineteen	220-223
Malefic symbols, or numbers, Sixteen	219
Mastery, The numbers of (2, 5, 7, 8, 9, 11, 22)	209
Marriage, Combinations of number vibrations in	93
Marriage, Causes of unhappy	98
Marriage, Complementary	105
Marriage, Law of opposites in	98
Marriage, Matching symbolscopes for	118
Marriage, Names, the secret in	108
Marriage, Right and True	93
Marriage, Types of inharmony in	100
Marriage, Vibrations which women and men gain or lose by	118

INDEX

Men, The ruling passions of	132
Mental vibrations, (1, 4, 7, and 8)	192
"Misfits"	202
Months, The	252
Months, The classified	255
Money, How to attract	262
Mystical Interpretation of numbers	25-26
Names and consciousness	28
Names and the cosmic law	230
Names to harmonize with play or work	122
Names come from, Where our	31
Negative and positive numbers (quality of consciousness)	170, 269
"Nick-names," The meaning of	130
Nine as an intensified number	129
Nine as a power number	212
Nineteen	223
Novitiate Consciousness, The, (The One, 1, 2, 3)	45
Novitiate—initiate—illuminati, An example of	51
Numbers and Letters, Table of	28
Numbers and Letters, Origin of	27
Numbers, Definition of	23
Numerology, Definition of	21, 36, 277
Odd and even numbers	231
Odd and even numbers (The Great Within and Without)	70
One, The	22
One, The, (The First Degree, 1, 2, 3)	45
One, The, the Many, the All	43, 125
Opposites, The Law of	98, 123, 237
Opposites in marriage, The law of	98
Outer vibrations	73
Outside, or even numbers	231
Periodicity, The Law of, (Cycles)	79

INDEX

Personal action in the year of (1, 2, 3, 4, 5, 6, 7, 8, 9, 11, 22) 255-257
Personality, or what we look like 52, 170
Personality, The importance of 170
Personality example, A 54
Personality, positive and negative,
    One 170
    Two 172
    Three 173
    Four 174
    Five 175
    Six 175
    Seven 176
    Eight 176
    Nine 177
    Eleven 178
    Twenty-two 178
Personality, Special numbers, 2, 3, 5, 7, 11, and 22   180
Pet names and their meanings 130
Physical and mental effect of name vibrations 121
Physical vibrations, (2-5) 191
Places, Names and, with example 233
Planes of Expression, The 189
Planets and numbers 130
Planets, How to determine your 130
Position of a number in the name, Influence of the 191, 214
Positive and Negative numbers, (quality of consciousness) 170, 269
Power, Necessary position of a letter for 218
Precipitates, The meaning of 82
Profession, Choosing a 237
Rebirth and the Nine Initiations 62
Registrations, or reflections of substance 23

294

INDEX

Reconstructive numbers 216
Repetition of letters in names, The meaning of...65, 131
Resistance, The line of least............................ 228
Ruling passions of humanity, The 132
Ruling passions, An example of 133
Ruling passions

of men		of women	
1	135	1	150
2	136	2	152
3	138	3	153
4	140	4	155
5	141	5	157
6	142	6	158
7	143	7	160
8	144	8	162
9	145	9	163
11	146	11	165
22	148	22	166

Self, The four divisions of................................ 52
Seven as an intensified number........................ 128
Seven as a power number................................ 211
Signatures, Business 264
Similars, opposites and complementaries............. 93
Situations, places and things........................... 233
Sixteen 219
Soul numbers 55, 134
Soul numbers, An example of........................... 57
Soul number in vocations, The influence of......... 234
Soul power as revealed in names..................... 55
Soul's Refrain, A 281
Special numbers.. 180
Spiritual vibrations (9-11) 193
Sunday of Life, The....................................... 126
Superfluous names 110

INDEX

Supravert, The	70, 73, 77
Symbolscope, An example of a	275
Symbolscope, How to interpret a	274
Symbolscope, How to write a	270
Symbolscope for Marriage, Matching	118
Test vibrations (initial and final)	124
Three, as an intensified number	128
Third Degree, The (8, 9, 11, and 22)	49
Thirteen	223
Things, Names of	236
Transition numbers	126
Twenty-two, as a power number	213
Two, as a power number	210
Two brothers, The (illus. Within and Without)	72
True Self, The	52
In destiny vibrations	59
In initiation vibrations	62
In personality vibrations	52
In soul vibrations	55
Unlucky, or Reconstructive numbers	218
Ultimate, or final, letters of names	125
Vibrations and accomplishments	64
Vibrations and numbers	25
Vibrations, cosmic	37
Vibrations, The source of	121
Vibrations, Table of	28
Vocations	191
Vocations and inner vibrations	60
Vocations, numbers and success	59-61
Vocation numbers (One to 22)	204-208
Vocational symbol	59
Vowels as symbols of soul power	55
Wedding day, month, hour and desires	111, 117
What we look like (Personality)	168

INDEX

Where our names come from.................................. 31
Women, The ruling passions of........................... 150
Year by year (1 to 12)......................................243-252
Years are numbered, How your........................... 237
Year vibrations, The importance of..................... 241
Year vibration, How to adjust yourself to any...... 240
Year vibration, How to ascertain your own............ 243
Year vibration means, What each
    One 243   Seven 247
    Two 243   Eight 248
    Three 244   Nine 249
    Four 244   Ten 250
    Five 245   Eleven 250
    Six 246   Twelve 251
Your numbers and vocations................................ 204